W9-DES-968

ISLANDS OF THE MEDITERRANEAN

MEDITERRANEAN CUISINE

ISLANDS OF THE MEDITERRANEAN

MEDITERRANEAN CUISINE

KÖNEMANN

Contents

List of Recipes

Level of difficulty:

*	Easy
**	Medium
***	Difficult

Hot & Cold Appetizers 8

Soups 40

Vegetarian Dishes 66

Fish & Seafood 90

Meat & Poultry 124

Desserts & Pastries 154

Hot & Cold Appetizers

Caponata

Preparation time: *45 minutes*
Cooking time: *40 minutes*
Difficulty: ★

Serves 4

4	eggplants (aubergines)
1/3 cup/80 ml	olive oil
1	carrot
1	celery heart
2	onions
2	tomatoes
1 bunch	parsley
1/2 cup/100 g	capers
1 cup/200 g	pitted green olives
1/2 cup/100 g	sun-dried tomatoes
2 tbsp/30 ml	wine vinegar
1 tbsp/15 g	superfine sugar
	salt and pepper

For the garnish:

parsley

Caponata, a Sicilian specialty made with eggplants, captures the essence of the Mediterranean sun. Similar to ratatouille, this easily made classic uses summer vegetables and has a distinctive sweet-sour taste.

Theories differ as to the origins of the name *caponata*. Some Sicilians believe that it is derived from the word *caupone*, or harbor-side tavern, where dishes of octopus, celery, and eggplant were traditionally prepared in a sweet-sour sauce.

The word may also refer to the fishermen of Naples, the *caponi*, who used to cook a kind of fish and vegetable soup while out at sea in their fishing boats.

One thing is certain: *caponata* is the universally popular trademark dish of Sicily's coastal regions.

Made from summer vegetables, typically the ingredients of *caponata* are tomatoes, onions, celery, and, most importantly, eggplants. Eggplants are particularly appreciated on Sicily and in southern Italy, where they are traditionally said to have been introduced by the Arabs in the 10th century. They can also be served stuffed with tomatoes, or pulped and shaped into balls or patties. *Macaroni alla Norma*, a pasta specialty from the area around Catania, is served with a topping of fried eggplant and ricotta cheese.

Famous for their excellent quality, capers from the nearby islands of Lipari and Pantelleria are another typical Sicilian ingredient. These are the flower buds of the caper bush, and are used in *caponata* to bring out the flavors of the other ingredients. They are usually sold preserved in vinegar, and should be rinsed before use.

Peel and dice the eggplants. Put them in a colander and salt generously. Leave to "sweat" for around 40 minutes, then rinse and pat dry (this removes the bitterness). Cook them in 4 tbsp of olive oil, on a medium heat, for about 10 minutes, stirring occasionally.

Peel and grate the carrot. Wash the celery and chop finely. Peel and chop the onions. Peel and pulp the fresh tomatoes (drop them briefly into a pan of just-boiled water before peeling). Wash and chop the parsley.

Gently brown the onions in a frying pan, in the remaining olive oil. Add the celery and soften over a low heat. Add the pulped tomatoes and mix them in. Add salt and pepper.

Now add the carrots to the mixture, together with the capers, the olives cut into slices, the chopped sun-dried tomatoes, and the parsley. Mix together and cook for about 10 minutes.

Add the diced eggplant and cook for a further 10 minutes.

Mix in the vinegar and the sugar. Cook for about 5 minutes. Serve garnished with chopped parsley.

Two Cretan Dishes

Preparation time: *20 minutes*
Cooking time for boubouristi snails: *30 minutes*
Cooking time for snails with fennel: *40 minutes*
Difficulty: ★

Serves 4

For the *boubouristi* snails with rosemary:

1 lb/500 g	live *petit-gris* snails
2/3 cup/150 ml	virgin olive oil
3 1/2 tbsp/50 g	fresh rosemary
2/3–4/5 cup/150–200 ml	vinegar
	salt

For the snails with fennel:

1 lb/500 g	live *petit-gris* snails
6	scallions (spring onions)
4/5 cup/200 ml	virgin olive oil
4/5 cup/200 ml	white wine
2 lb/1 kg	fennel tops
4	ripe tomatoes
	salt and pepper

For the garnish:

fennel tops

Many Cretans still observe the requirement to fast on certain days in the Christian calendar. With meat from warm-blooded animals, eggs, and dairy produce off the menu, the "fast" typically features fresh vegetables, snails, beans, and olives. Archaeological excavations on the neighboring island of Santorini have revealed that snails were already being eaten in the Minoan period. The ancient Greeks also ate these easily harvested delicacies.

The snails of the Cretan mountains favor a habitat of aromatic plants that gives them their celebrated flavor. The Cretans gather them and keep them in boxes containing vine shoots for two weeks. They are then carefully cleaned and, if necessary, the operculum (the bony covering on the snail's "foot") is removed. From among the many Cretan recipes for snails, Ioannis Lappas has selected *boubouristi* (fried) snails, generally served as an appetizer, and snails with fennel, a main dish.

The most popular way of serving snails on Crete is fried (*boubouristi*). Fried snails are one of the island's favorite *meze*, accompanying a glass of wine or the local brandy, *tsikoudia*. The live snails (in their shells) are arranged in a pan on a thin layer of salt, with the shell openings facing downward. All the shells should touch the bottom of the pan to ensure even cooking. As the cooking proceeds, the snails release their juice and shrink into their shells, but not before their flesh has become impregnated with the salt, resulting in a crisp crust. The Cretans often dip *dakos*, the delicious local bread, into the juices.

In the second recipe given here, the snails are cooked with *marathos*, the fragrant wild fennel that grows in the rocky countryside of Crete. This use of wild herbs is typical of Cretan cooking. If fennel tops are unobtainable, they can be substituted with dill, which has a very similar taste.

Wash the snails thoroughly under running water or in a bowl to clean them of any dirt. Remove the operculum if necessary.

For the boubouristi *snails: cover the bottom of a heavy frying pan with a layer of salt and place the snails on it, in their shells. Heat the pan quickly until a greenish-yellow "juice" is released. Add the oil and toss over a high heat for 5 minutes.*

Add the rosemary. Douse the snails with the vinegar. Continue tossing the snails until the vinegar has evaporated, and serve immediately.

using Snails

For snails with fennel: fill a saucepan with water and bring to the boil. Immerse the live snails, boil for 2 minutes and drain them.

Chop the onions. In a pan, toss the scallions and snails in oil for 5 minutes over a high heat. Add the white wine, salt, and pepper and stir over the heat for a further 3–4 minutes.

Snip the fennel tops finely and chop the tomatoes into small dice. Add these to the snails and cook for 30 minutes (add a little more water, if needed, during cooking). Serve hot, garnished with fresh fennel tops.

Estopeta of Cod

Desalting of cod: *overnight*
Preparation time: *20 minutes*
Difficulty: ★

Serves 4

1 lb/400 g	salt cod fillet
2	ripe tomatoes
½	onion
2	scallions (spring onions)
1 tbsp/15 g	parsley
1 tsp/5 g	paprika
4 oz/100 g	macerated (*marcidas*) black olives
⅔ cup/150 ml	Sóller virgin olive oil

In the Balearic Islands, as in all parts of Spain, salt cod has been a staple feature of home cooking for many centuries. *Estopeta*, a mixture of flaked salt cod, pulped tomatoes, onions, and herbs, is one of the country's oldest cod dishes. Regarded as old-fashioned and homely, it is rarely found on restaurant menus. Unusually, Oscar Martínez Plaza regularly serves *estopeta* to diners at his restaurant in Palma de Mallorca. In fact, this very simple and economical recipe produces a delicious, refined dish fit for any occasion.

A successful *estopeta* requires salt cod and olive oil of the very best quality. Salt cod should always be thoroughly desalted by soaking overnight in several changes of cold water. This is especially important for *estopeta*, for which the cod is used uncooked. The fish should be left to soak in a bowl of water in the refrigerator. Change the water every three hours or so, and first thing in the morning after an overnight soaking. Oscar Martínez Plaza recommends chopping the cod into small strips before soaking to assist the desalting process.

Olives and olive oil form the basis of a delicious sauce that complements the flavor of the raw salt fish. Olive trees have been grown on terraces in the Sierra de Tramuntana region of Mallorca since the 16th century. The Sóller cooperative produces a particularly fine, golden yellow extra-virgin olive oil with low acidity.

Balearic olives are ripe for harvesting in October. Black and slightly wrinkled, they have a strong scent. Those that are not turned into oil are often macerated in vinegar with bay leaves, garlic, and lemon. These *aceitunas marcidas* melt in the mouth and add a wonderful taste to *estopeta*.

Rinse the salt cod fillets and cut them away from the skin into fine strips. Immerse the strips in a bowl of cold water and leave to soak for 24 hours (see the notes on desalting, above).

Skin the tomatoes by slicing into the skin around the middle, and placing them in a pan of just-boiled water. When the skin begins to detach itself, remove them to a bowl of cold water. When cool, remove the skin with the point of a knife.

Peel and chop the onion. Remove the roots from the scallions and chop them finely with the parsley. Chop up the peeled tomatoes.

with Macerated Olives

Drain the cod and place it in a mixing bowl. Add the parsley and scallions.

Next add the chopped onion, paprika, and chopped tomatoes (keeping back a little for garnishing).

Remove the pits and chop the olives to form a paste. Mix them in a bowl with the olive oil. Shape the cod mixture into rounds on individual serving plates (use a bottomless, circular metal mold, or a large pastry cutter). Garnish with the olive sauce and crushed tomato.

Zucchini Flowers

Preparation time: *40 minutes*
Cooking time: *25 minutes*
Difficulty: ★★

Serves 4

16	small zucchini with their flowers
1 lb/500 g	monkfish tail
2	leeks
4/5 cup/200 ml	olive oil
1 1/4 cups/300 ml	white wine
3	tomatoes, skinned
2 cups/500 ml	fish bouillon
2 tbsp/30 g	cornstarch
	salt

Zucchini flowers are a relatively new culinary discovery on the Balearic Islands, thanks to a number of local chefs who have looked abroad for inspiration. Usually, the flowers are detached from the zucchini, dipped in flour and fried. The following recipe, created by Bartolomé-Jaime Trias Luis, proposes a tasty stuffing of monkfish, tomatoes, and leeks simmered in white wine.

The zucchini flowers are very fragile and must be cleaned with great care. Gently part the petals and pull out the pistil. The petals should not be opened out completely or they will tear. Keep the flowers wrapped and refrigerated until required or they will soon wilt.

Monkfish is a popular Mediterranean fish with a delicate taste. It is common in the waters around the Balearic Islands. In many countries, the ugly head is removed before the fish is offered for sale. Other fish suitable for this recipe include bass, dentex, and sea bream.

The finished stuffing should always be cooled in the refrigerator before placing it in an icing bag with a small tip. It can then be piped into the flowers.

Allow about three stuffed flowers (with their zucchini) per person. The stuffed flowers and zucchini can be presented lying flat on top of the sauce, or standing "upright" with the petals tucked underneath. The stuffing can be eaten immediately, at this stage, with a teaspoon. However, Bartolomé-Jaime Trias Luis recommends baking the stuffed flowers with their zucchini, so that the complementary flavors and textures of the crispy petals, zucchini flesh, and stuffing can be enjoyed at their very best.

Carefully remove the pistil from the center of the zucchini flowers. Remove the zucchini stalks by cutting diagonally across the end of the vegetables.

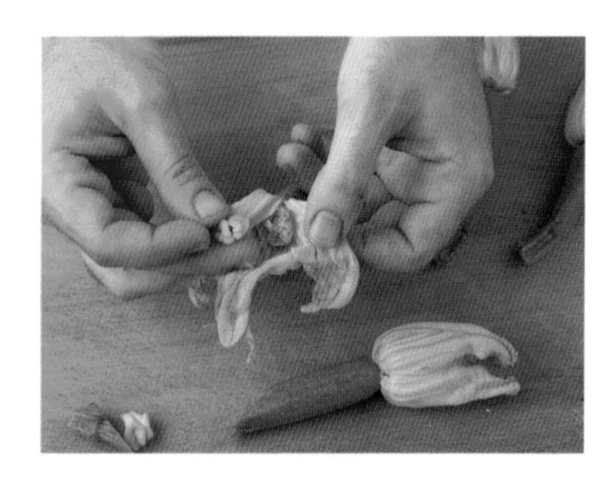

Clean, skin, and rinse the monkfish tail. Remove the bone and chop the flesh into strips, then into tiny dice (ask your fishmonger to do this, if you prefer).

To make the stuffing, lightly brown the chopped leeks in oil, then add the white wine and allow it to evaporate over a high heat. Chop 1 tomato and add to the leeks. Let it reduce, adding a little more white wine if necessary. Remove from the heat. Pulp the remaining 2 tomatoes.

Stuffed with Monkfish

Add the cubed fish to the pan with a little salt. Cook for 5 minutes over a high heat.

Pour 1¼ cups/300 ml of the fish bouillon into the stuffing mixture. Combine the remaining ¾ cup/185 ml with the cornstarch and add this to the mixture, stirring as it cooks and thickens. Check the seasoning and leave to cool.

Fill an icing bag with the stuffing and pipe it into the zucchini flowers. Close the petals. The stuffed flowers may be served immediately, garnished with the pulped tomatoes (eat the stuffing with a teaspoon); or heat them for 10 minutes at 320 °F/160 °C and serve warm.

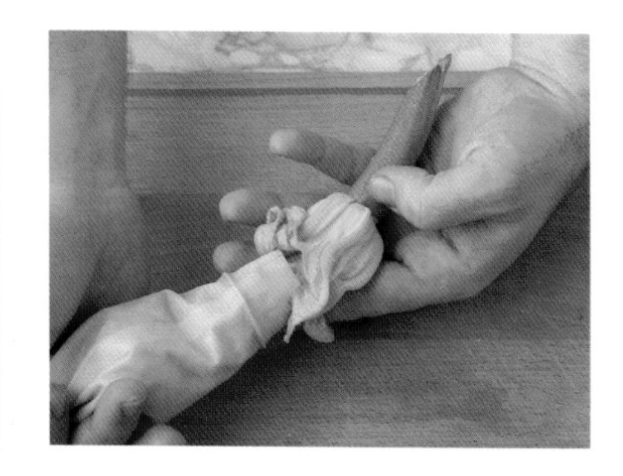

Octopus

Preparation time: *30 minutes*
Cooking time: *1 hour 5 minutes*
Difficulty: ★

Serves 4

1 lb/500 g	octopus
4/5 cup/200 ml	red wine
2 oz/50 g	onion
1 clove	garlic
2 cups/100 g	fresh breadcrumbs
4 tsp/20 g	parsley
4 tsp/20 g	dill
7/8 cup/100 g	flour
	salt and pepper
	olive oil for frying

Balls of ground and fried octopus meat, *kleftedes*, are eaten during Holy Week on Crete. Generally found as a *meze*, served with aperitifs, they may be accompanied by a tomato sauce or may simply be decorated with slices of tomato and lemon.

The islanders of Crete (especially people living on or near the coast) eat plenty of fish and seafood. Scorpion fish, cuttlefish, and octopus are particular favorites. Of the different cephalopods, only octopus is suitable for making *kleftedes*: squid is not sufficiently fleshy, and cuttlefish is too firm. Choose a plump octopus with plenty of tentacles.

The Cretans use a strong, perfumed light red or rosé wine when cooking octopus. If the liquid dries during cooking, add a little water. When the octopus is tender, drain off the liquid and remove the violet membrane covering the flesh.

For delicious *kleftedes*, Michalis Markakis suggests freezing the octopus overnight, after it has been cooked. This will give a perfect texture for grinding and shaping the next day. The flesh can also be ground immediately after cooking, but its texture will be softer and more elastic.

These *kleftedes* are flavored with dill and flat-leaf parsley: the most popular herbs in Greece. Dill, or *anithos* in Greek, has straight, hollow stems and umbrella-shaped clusters of flowers similar to those of aniseed and fennel. The ancient Greeks used the flowers and seeds of the dill plant for cooking and medicinal purposes.

The addition of a little olive oil and vinegar to the mixture will make it softer, tastier, and easier to handle.

Rinse the octopus under running water. Place it in a casserole dish and brown it in the oil, keeping it covered until it changes to a red color. Add the wine, replace the lid and cook on a medium to low heat for 45 minutes.

Clean and skin the cooked octopus. Cut the tentacles into chunks. Place the meat in a food processor and blend to a smooth paste.

Transfer the octopus paste to a bowl. Add the chopped onion and garlic, salt, pepper, and breadcrumbs.

Kleftedes

Finally, add the chopped parsley and dill. Work the mixture with your fingertips to ensure that the ingredients are well integrated.

Take small lumps of the mixture and roll them in the palm of the hand to make plum-sized balls.

Pour the flour onto a plate and roll the balls in it. Then deep fry them in very hot olive oil until golden. Drain them on absorbent paper and eat while still hot.

Serge Fazzini's

Preparation time: *15 minutes*
Cooking time: *25 minutes*
Difficulty: ★

Serves 4

½	fresh *figatellu* (Corsican pork liver sausage)
1 clove	garlic
½ stick/55 g	butter
3	eggs
1 cup/235 ml	milk
	a little olive oil
	salt and pepper

For the caramel:

5½ tbsp/180 g	superfine sugar
	a little honey vinegar
4 tsp/20 ml	Cap Corse (fortified wine)

Serge Fazzini's *figatellu* terrines are a highly original baked appetizer featuring a number of typically Corsican ingredients. This delicious sweet-sour dish is an affectionate homage to the produce of his native island.

Made using traditional methods, and still home-produced in the small inland villages, Corsican charcuterie is one of the jewels of the island's cuisine. The long list includes *figatellu* (pork liver sausage), *coppa*, and *prizzuttu* (ham).

Corsica's free-range pigs are a familiar sight on mountain roads. Sometimes crossed with wild boar, and feeding mainly on chestnuts, their meat has a particularly fine flavor. They are traditionally slaughtered at Christmas-time.

Homemade *figatellu* is a pure delight. The sausage is smoked over the *fucone* (the family hearth) for three or four days, after which it may be grilled (fresh *figatellu*), or left to dry in a well-ventilated room. It can be found in specialist delicatessens.

Combined here with butter, milk, and eggs, the fresh *figatellu* reveals all its rustic charm. Its Mediterranean origins are clear from the hint of garlic. Cultivated on the island for over 5,000 years, Corsica's strongly flavored garlic is available all year round. An essential ingredient of the island's cuisine, it is used both raw (finely chopped, for a strong flavor) and in cooked dishes (for a milder taste).

As an enthusiast for the specialties of his native Corsica, Serge Fazzini suggests finishing the *figatellu* terrines with a topping of caramelized sauce made with Cap Corse, a sweet, fortified wine (port or marsala are effective substitutes). Corsican *brocciu*, a soft cheese made from ewe's or goat's milk, makes a perfect accompaniment, sprinkled with *nepita*, the Corsican wild mint.

Using a knife, remove the skin from the fresh figatellu *sausage. Cut it into pieces and blend these in a food processor.*

Add the peeled garlic clove, melted butter, eggs, milk, salt, and pepper and process again.

Oil 4 ramekins with a brush dipped in olive oil. Divide the mixture between the ramekins.

Figatellu Terrines

Place the ramekins in an ovenproof dish. Carefully add water to cover the base of the dish. Place the dish in an oven heated to 350 °F/180 °C and cook for about 25 minutes. When cooked, leave the terrines to cool, then turn them out onto a plate.

To make the caramel, pour the sugar into a small saucepan. Add a little water and heat. When the mixture becomes syrupy, add the honey vinegar. Mix with a wooden spoon.

Pour the Cap Corse into the caramel mixture and stir thoroughly. Place a figatellu terrine on each plate and pour the sauce around it.

Pa Amb Oli

Preparation time: *10 minutes*
Cooking time: *30 minutes*
Difficulty: ★

Serves 4

1 loaf	country-style bread
1 tsp/5 g	paprika
	Sóller virgin olive oil
½ cup/100 g	sun-dried tomatoes
7 oz/200 g	Mahón-Menorca cheese

1	scallion (spring onion)
1 clove	garlic
½ cup/100 g	*marcidas* black olives
1	tomato, finely diced (optional)
a few sprigs	parsley (optional)
	salt

For the garnish:

	Sóller virgin olive oil
1 clove	garlic
1	scallion (spring onion)

Pa amb oli (bread with oil) is simple, economical, and a perennial favorite with the people of the Balearic Islands. In its simplest form, *pa amb oli* consists of nothing more than good, fresh bread sprinkled with salt and dipped in top-quality olive oil. For a more substantial dish, Bartolomé-Jaime Trias Luis has added sun-dried tomatoes, cheese, and herbs to the bread, which he serves with an olive sauce.

The bread used for this dish should be of the best quality. The locals favor *pan pagès*, a firm, white country-style bread with a thick brown crust. It has the advantage of remaining fresh and moist for several days.

The dried tomatoes used in this recipe are still prepared on Menorca in the traditional way, by the older women. Whole tomatoes are put in a pot with a little water and placed near a source of heat for 6–8 hours. When the water has evaporated and the tomatoes have dried out, they are allowed to cool and are then peeled.

Slivers of Mahón-Menorca cheese are placed over the tomatoes. This most famous of the Balearic cheeses is produced on Menorca, a verdant island famed since ancient times for the quality of its cattle. Made from unpasteurized milk, it is sometimes coated with oil and paprika to prolong its life.

The black olives should be pitted, chopped, and mixed with the oil to make a sauce. *Marcidas* olives are gathered from the ground after the olive harvest and have a distinctive, wrinkled skin. They are macerated in a mixture of herbs and spices, and blend beautifully with the olive oil produced in the town of Sóller (Bartolomé-Jaime Trias Luis's birthplace) on Mallorca. Sóller's olive oil is reputed to be the best in the Balearics.

Remove the bread crust and cut the bread into regular slices about ¾ inch/1.5 cm thick, and then into rectangles 4 inches/10 cm by 1 inch/2–3 cm wide. Brown the pieces of bread for 10 minutes in an oven heated to 350 °F/180 °C.

Arrange the pieces of toasted bread on a plate. Sprinkle with paprika and salt, then drizzle with a little olive oil.

Arrange the dried tomatoes on each piece of toast so that they overlap slightly. Drizzle on some more oil.

with Cheese

Remove the rind from the Mahón-Menorca cheese and cut into thin slivers. Arrange these over the dried tomatoes.

Pour a little oil into a pan and heat it to a low temperature. Add the finely chopped fresh garlic and scallion and cook them very gently for 20 minutes until transparent and just golden.

Remove the pits from the olives and chop them. Mix with the olive oil. Prepare each plate with a line of olive sauce, diced fresh tomato, and 2–3 parsley leaves. Garnish the toasted bread with the garlic and scallion mixture, drizzling a little more oil over the whole.

Sicilian

Preparation time: *25 minutes*
Cooking time: *20 minutes*
Difficulty: ★

Serves 4

4	red bell peppers
2 cups/400 g	tomatoes
2 cloves	garlic
1 bunch	basil
1½ cups/150 g	dried/toasted breadcrumbs
3½ oz/100 g	grated pecorino cheese
3½ tbsp/50 ml	olive oil
	salt and pepper

For the garnish:

basil
grated pecorino
olive oil

Sicilian stuffed peppers, although a very simple dish, are a treat for the taste buds. A Mediterranean classic, using typical local ingredients, they are generally eaten cold in the summertime.

Red bell peppers are appreciated for their mild taste and grow plentifully all over Sicily. Their thick and very sweet flesh is ideal for this recipe. Before stuffing, it is important to cook them in the oven for 20 minutes. This will make them easy to peel. For even more color, use yellow and orange bell peppers too. Select peppers that are firm and smooth-skinned, without black marks or other blemishes, and with a stalk that is still green and rigid.

Carefully concocted stuffings are a feature of many Sicilian dishes. The crunchy texture of oven-dried breadcrumbs adds character to the stuffed peppers.

The presence of sun-drenched ingredients such as garlic, basil, and, of course, olive oil in this dish is typical of Mediterranean island cooking. Sicily is the most important center of olive production in Italy, with some 445,000 acres/180,000 hectares devoted to the cultivation of a huge range of varieties including *biancolilla*, *moresca*, *nocella etnea*, and *tonda iblea*. Sicilian olive oil is characterized by its deliciously full and fruity flavor with an aftertaste of sweet almonds.

The rolled, stuffed peppers are even more delicious when combined with pecorino cheese. Very popular in the southern regions of Italy, this ewe's-milk cheese blends particularly well with the other ingredients. Parmesan makes a good substitute if necessary.

Arrange the peppers in an ovenproof dish and salt them generously. Toast them in a moderate oven (350 °F/180 °C) or under the broiler for about 10 minutes. Turn them over and cook for a further 10 minutes.

Peel the peppers. Cut them in half lengthwise and remove the seeds.

For the stuffing, peel the tomatoes (see the method described for estopeta*, p.14) and remove the pits. Dice them small. Chop the garlic. Chop the basil leaves.*

Stuffed Peppers

In a bowl, mix the breadcrumbs, garlic, grated pecorino, basil, and tomatoes. Add salt and pepper and the olive oil. Mix with a wooden spoon.

Using the wooden spoon, carefully arrange the stuffing on the halves of pepper.

Roll the peppers up and arrange them on the plate. Garnish with basil, grated pecorino, and a little olive oil.

Beekeeper's

Preparation time:	*10 minutes*
Cooking time:	*10 minutes*
Difficulty:	★

Serves 4

1	curly endive lettuce
7 oz/200 g	*figatellu* (Corsican pork liver sausage)
2½ tbsp/40 ml	olive oil
4	very fresh eggs
¼ cup/60 ml	honey vinegar
	salt
	freshly ground pepper

For the dressing:

2 tbsp/30 ml	wine vinegar
2 level tbsp/60 g	*maquis* honey
7 tbsp/100 ml	olive oil
	salt and pepper

The island of Corsica is famous for the scent of the *maquis*, its unique wild scrub vegetation, including numerous hardy, aromatic herbs. Of the 2,300 species of plant identified on the island, 280 are found nowhere else. Rightly proud of this natural wealth, the Corsicans have always prized their local honey.

Easily prepared, this "beekeeper's salad" is a delicious appetizer that pays tribute to a couple of locally-produced specialties, with a finely balanced contrast between the sweet and savory ingredients.

Already famous in Antiquity, Corsican honey was especially prized by patrician Roman ladies, who used it to perfume their baths of asses' milk. Recently awarded a coveted *appellation d'origine contrôlée*, there are six different types of Corsican honey. For this recipe, Vincent Tabarani has chosen *maquis*.

Depending on the season, this nectar of the gods takes on different flavors. The honey harvested throughout Corsica in early May is particularly delicate. Amber in color, the bees gather it from white heather, lavender, and wild rosemary.

The honey produced in the summer—fruity and flowery in taste—comes from the high valleys, from a wide variety of wild flowering plants including thyme and broom. In the fall, the honey has a powerful, bitter taste. Often creamy in appearance, its woody scent recalls that of arbutus (Italy's famous strawberry tree) and chestnuts.

This delicious salad gives pride of place to Corsica's traditional *figatellu* smoked sausage, made from pork liver. Freshly made *figatelli* are eaten grilled, between two slices of bread or polenta made with chestnut flour. Other dried sausages or diced bacon are acceptable substitutes here.

Wash the lettuce and remove the green outer leaves. Finely chop the white leaves.

Prick the sausage and broil it for about 10 minutes.

Cut the sausage into equal slices.

Salad

For the dressing, pour the wine vinegar into a bowl and add salt and pepper. Beat in the maquis *honey with a fork. Add the olive oil. Set aside.*

Warm 2½ tbsp of olive oil in a pan. Break the eggs into the pan, adding salt and pepper, and fry them.

Pour the honey vinegar over the eggs. Deglaze. Arrange the salad on the plates with the eggs and the figatellu*. Season to taste.*

Tuna Bottarga Salad

Preparation time: *10 minutes*
Cooking time: *1 minute*
Difficulty: ✯

Serves 4

11 oz/300 g	fennel bulbs
	juice of 1 lemon
6 oz/180 g	*bottarga di tonno* (salted, dried red tuna fish roe)
4 oz/100 g	pitted black olives
1 tbsp/15 ml	olive oil
1 tbsp/15 ml	white wine vinegar

For the dressing:

4	oranges
2 tbsp/30 ml	olive oil

For the garnish:

	fennel seeds
4 sprigs	fennel tops

Sicily has a distinctive, ancient culture, and the feel of an island where time has stood still. A strong sense of family is only one of the many deeply rooted traditions that survive. In springtime at Favignia, near Trapani, thousands of spectators come to see the annual *mattanza*, when the local fishermen use traditional longboats and huge nets to trap and spear large numbers of tuna fish. A favorite dish in Sicily, these enormous fish can reach up to 12 feet/4 meters in length, and weigh several hundreds of pounds.

Giuseppe Barone's easily-made salad, using *bottarga di tonno*, oranges, and fennel, comes from Porto di Capo Passero, a small fishing village in the far south of the island. With its typically Sicilian ingredients, this cold appetizer is ideal for a summer menu. *Bottarga di tonno*, a local specialty, consists of the salted, pressed, and dried roe of the female tuna fish. Also known as "Sicilian caviar," it is served sliced. It can be eaten raw, fried, or steamed. In some recipes it is dressed with olive oil, garlic, parsley, and a little red pepper.

This refreshing, vitamin-rich salad is dressed with the sharp juice of oranges and features a delightful mixture of tastes and textures. The aniseed-flavored fennel provides an intriguing contrast to the other ingredients.

Famous since the Middle Ages for its citrus fruits, the countryside around Palermo resembles a magnificent orchard. Originally created by Arab colonizers in the 11th and 12th centuries, these fruit groves benefited from a sophisticated irrigation system. Many varieties of citrus fruit are grown on the island, the best known being the navel, *tarocco* (blood), and oval oranges.

For the dressing, cut away the peel of the oranges, juice them, strain, and put the juice to one side.

Wash the fennel bulbs and slice finely. Place the sliced fennel in a bowl of water to which lemon juice has been added.

Evenly slice the pressed tuna fish roe.

with Orange and Fennel

On a moderate heat, sauté the olives for 1 minute in a frying pan with olive oil. Add the vinegar.

Now finish the dressing: add one tbsp of hot water to the bowl of orange juice, together with the olive oil. Whisk until an emulsion is obtained.

Drain the fennel in a sieve. Arrange it on the plates with the bottarga*, the sautéed olives, and the orange dressing. Garnish with fennel seeds and fennel tops.*

Isabella Salad

Preparation time: *10 minutes*
Difficulty: ★

Serves 4

1	small celery heart
1	small tomato
4 oz/100 g	*bottarga* (mullet roe)

For the dressing:

1	lemon
2 tbsp/30 ml	olive oil
	freshly ground pepper

For the garnish:

celery leaves

This flavor-filled salad is a variation on a classic of Sardinian cuisine. Created by Amerigo Murgia, he has named it after his daughter Isabella. Very easy to prepare, it makes a delicious summertime appetizer.

Surrounded by a turquoise sea of crystalline purity, Sardinia is the most distant of the Italian islands. The traditional dishes of this ravishingly beautiful island are generally very simple. A particularly well-known specialty is *bottarga di muggine* (mullet roe).

Found and fished mainly off the coast around Cabras in the west of the island, mullet has a distinctive flavor. The *bottarga* is generally prepared in August and September when the female fish are full of eggs. The elongated roe sack is removed, salted, and massaged by hand, before being pressed between wooden planks beneath stone or marble weights. The roe is then air-dried for between four and eight weeks, turning a rich amber in color.

Bottarga is much prized in Sardinian cuisine, often simply eaten in thin slices on fresh bread. It can be mixed with olive oil and scattered in crumbs over pasta. An essential ingredient for this recipe, it can be found in Italian or other delicatessens as well as in specialist grocers. Amerigo Murgia suggests that it is best placed in the freezer for a few minutes to make it easier to slice.

Celery is used to enhance this refreshing appetizer, with its crunchy texture and hint of aniseed. This recipe provides a perfect opportunity to get acquainted with the sun-filled riches of Sardinian cuisine.

Wash the celery heart. Cut it into fine slices.

Place the tomato in boiling water for a few moments, peel, and cut into small, even dice.

Cut the bottarga *into thin slices of equal size.*

with Bottarga

Squeeze the lemon, removing any pits from the juice.

Prepare the salad dressing by first grinding some pepper into a bowl. Now add the olive oil, followed by the lemon juice. Mix.

Assemble the individual salads using a bottomless circular metal mold placed on each plate: start with a layer of celery. Cover this with some bottarga*, then a layer of tomato. Repeat the 3 layers. Remove the circle. Pour over the dressing. Garnish with celery leaves.*

Spaghetti with Bottarga

Preparation time: *10 minutes*
Cooking time: *10 minutes*
Difficulty: ★

Serves 4

1 oz/25 g	*bottarga* (mullet roe)
½ lb/250 g	shrimp
½ bunch	parsley
1 clove	garlic
8 tbsp/120 ml	olive oil
1 lb/500 g	spaghetti
	salt

For the garnish:
parsley

A native of Sardinia, and an enthusiast for the island's cooking and produce, Amerigo Murgia insists that the best *bottarga* of all is Sardinian. This national specialty, made from salted and dried mullet roe, is particularly popular on the Italian islands. One of the nicest ways to eat it is combined with spaghetti and shrimp, for a quintessentially maritime Mediterranean dish.

Bottarga di muggine, a typical dish of the coastal areas of Sardinia, was traditionally eaten in winter. Today, it can be found all year round in specialist grocers. It should be an attractive amber in color. According to the chef, a paler color means that the eggs have not been dried for long enough. If the color is too dark, the *bottarga* is too old.

The female mullet, caught toward the end of the summer off the coast near Cabras, are fished solely for their eggs. The sacs containing the eggs are salted and pressed between two wooden boards, before being left to dry for three or four months, by which time they will have acquired a smooth paste-like consistency. This Sardinian "caviar" is available vacuum packed, and may be rectangular in shape.

Often combined with spaghetti or other long pasta such as linguine, *bottarga* has a unique taste. The recipe given here is very simple to prepare and can be served as an appetizer or a main dish.

The Sardinian coast, a veritable paradise for fishermen, is famed for its pure waters and countless fish, shellfish, and crustacea. Octopuses, crabs, and shrimp are found in abundance, and the latter are particularly sought after for their delicate flavor. Shrimp are used to complete this recipe, but langoustines (Dublin Bay prawns) would be an acceptable substitute.

Finely grate the bottarga.

Remove the shrimp shells and cut the shrimp into three. Wash and chop the parsley. Peel the garlic and crush it.

Heat the olive oil in a pan and add the crushed garlic and the parsley. Add the shelled shrimp and sauté them for a few minutes.

and Shrimp

Bring a pot of water to the boil. When boiling, add salt and the spaghetti. Cook for about 9 minutes.

Remove the spaghetti and transfer to the pan containing the shrimp mixture. Shake the pan to mix.

Tip the grated bottarga *over the pasta and shake again to mix it in. Serve the pasta with a garnish of chopped parsley.*

Spaghetti with

Preparation time: *20 minutes*
Cooking time: *1 hour 10 minutes*
Difficulty: ★★

Serves 8

4	rabbit heads
	olive oil
3	medium onions
3	bay leaves
2 or 3	chiles
8 cloves	garlic
3/4 cup/200 g	tomato concentrate
1 lb/500 g	canned peeled tomatoes
4	rabbit livers
4	rabbit kidneys
1	small carrot
1/4 cup/50 g	fresh shelled peas
1 1/4 lb/600 g	spaghetti
	grated parmesan
	salt and pepper

In 1530, Emperor Charles V graciously presented the island of Malta to the Knights of St John of Jerusalem. They made the island the headquarters of their Order, building churches, fortresses, and palaces and founding the city that was to become the capital, Valletta. In the 16th century, wild rabbits were found in all parts of the island. To reserve this source of meat for themselves, the knights banned the local Maltese from hunting them. Anyone caught poaching was condemned to row in the galleys.

This traditional, economical pasta dish makes use of those parts of the rabbit that are not used in *fenek moqli*, a delicious dish of rabbit sautéed with garlic and white wine generally regarded as the national dish of Malta.

The rabbit heads are boiled with sliced onion to make a bouillon that is the basis of the sauce. Rosemary may also be added with the bay leaf. When the bouillon has simmered for at least 45 minutes, it should be strained and combined with the prepared tomato mixture. Alternatively, it can simply be strained through a sieve placed over the pan containing the sauce.

The Maltese love tomatoes just as much as the Italians do. Tomatoes are a staple ingredient in Maltese cooking, and there are a number of local varieties including the enormous segmented "beef tomato." Tomatoes are used to prepare *hobz biz-zejt*, a kind of sandwich of country bread with tomatoes, mint, capers, and olive oil.

Malta is only 58 miles/93 km across the sea from Sicily, so it is not surprising that pasta has become an important part of the Maltese diet. A range of pastas closely resembling those found in Italy is produced here.

Brown the rabbit heads for 5 minutes in the oil. Add 1 chopped onion and continue cooking for a few minutes.

Pour some cold water over the rabbit heads. Add the bay leaves. Bring to the boil and simmer for 45 minutes.

Meanwhile, chop the 2 onions, the chiles, and the garlic, and brown them in olive oil in a large saucepan. Add the tomato concentrate and cook for 3 minutes, stirring. Finely chop the tomatoes and add them with salt and pepper. Cook for another 3–4 minutes.

Rabbit

Strain the bouillon and add it to the saucepan containing the tomato sauce.

Chop the livers, kidneys, and carrot into small regular-sized dice.

Add the liver, kidney, carrot, and peas to the tomato sauce and cook for 8 minutes. During this time, cook the spaghetti for 8 minutes in boiling water. Drain the pasta and mix with the tomato sauce. Add some olive oil and grated parmesan, and serve.

Storzapretti

Preparation time: *40 minutes*
Cooking time: *25 minutes*
Difficulty: ★

Serves 4

11 oz/300 g	Swiss chard leaves
1	*brocciu* (Corsican cheese, weighing about 14 oz or 400 g)
2	eggs
3 pinches	*nepita* (peppery wild mint)
1/3 cup/20 g	fresh breadcrumbs (optional)
7/8 cup/100 g	flour
3 1/2 oz/100 g	grated *tomme* (Corsican cheese)
	salt and pepper

For the tomato sauce:

1/2	onion
2 tbsp/30 ml	olive oil
1 clove	garlic
1/2 bunch	parsley
4	tomatoes
	salt and pepper

Corsican cooking is both generous and substantial, and traditionally features entirely local produce. *Storzapretti* are a good example. According to legend, the name of this specialty refers to a particularly greedy priest who ate large quantities of these vegetarian dumplings every day. This easy recipe is usually served as a hot appetizer. For a main dish simply double the quantities.

This dish uses the famous Corsican *brocciu*, a mild, creamy cheese. *Brocciu* is made on local farms in the winter and spring; the similar-tasting French cheese known as *brousse* is an acceptable substitute if *brocciu* is unavailable. Another important ingredient is Swiss chard. Blanched for a few minutes and then finely chopped, these leaves combine extremely well with the *brocciu*. Swiss chard, a fresh and nutritious vegetable, is grown in small inland gardens, and sold in large quantities in the springtime. Choose young plants for their milder flavor, and wash them carefully before cooking. Spinach leaves can be substituted for the Swiss chard if necessary.

With the addition of *nepita*, a slightly peppery wild mint, these *storzapretti* instantly evoke the *maquis* (wild scrub) that is so important a feature of the Corsican landscape. This very typical dish is finished with the characteristic taste of Corsican *tomme*. *Tomme* is a strong ewe's-milk cheese, the taste of which underlines the rustic origins of this specialty.

Clean the Swiss chard leaves. Heat a pan of salted water to boiling point and add the leaves, cooking them for 2 minutes. Drain and chop.

For the sauce, lightly brown the chopped onion in the olive oil. Add the garlic and chopped parsley. Add the chopped tomatoes with salt and pepper. Cook over a gentle heat for about 20 minutes. Mix together and set aside.

Crumble the brocciu *into a bowl and add the chopped Swiss chard and the eggs. Season with salt and pepper. Sprinkle on the* nepita *and mix in. If the mixture is too liquid, add some breadcrumbs.*

with Corsican Cheeses

Form the mixture into dumplings and roll them in flour.

Heat a pot of salted water to boiling point. Now carefully lower the dumplings into the water with a spatula. When they rise to the surface, lift them out.

Pour the tomato sauce into an ovenproof dish and place the dumplings in it. Sprinkle the grated Corsican tomme *over the dish and brown it for 5 minutes in an oven heated to 400 °F/200 °C. Serve.*

Tonn Immellah with

Preparation time:	*30 minutes*
Cooking time:	*2–2½ hours*
Soaking time for garbanzo beans:	*overnight*
Difficulty:	★

Serves 4

4 slices	Maltese country bread
7 oz/200 g	salted tuna
7 tbsp/100 ml	olive oil

For the garbanzo purée:

1 cups/200 g	garbanzo beans (chickpeas)
3 cloves	garlic
4	anchovy fillets in oil
½ bunch	flat-leaf parsley
3½ tbsp/50 ml	olive oil
	salt and pepper

For the tomato salad:

2	large tomatoes
8 leaves	basil
½ bunch	flat-leaf parsley
3 cloves	garlic
½	red onion
1 tbsp/15 g	capers
3½ tbsp/50 ml	olive oil
	salt and pepper

Optional garnish:

	arugola leaves (rocket)

Michael Cauchi is the owner and chef of a noted fish restaurant, *Il Re del Pesce*, in Marsacala on the island of Malta. As an appetizer, he suggests these slices of salted tuna served with garbanzo purée, and an anchovy and tomato salad on toasted bread.

Tuna is one of the most commonly-found species of fish caught in the waters around Malta. Michael Cauchi likes to oven-bake the fresh fish, serving it with a caper or sweet-sour sauce. Salted tuna, as used in our recipe, is sold in pieces, either whole or ready-sliced. It is ready to eat and is a perfect accompaniment for cold vegetable dishes.

To make the accompanying garbanzo purée, it is important to soak the dried beans in water overnight and then boil them for two to two-and-a-half hours (or until soft). When blending them in the food processor, add a little of the cooking liquid as necessary to give a creamy consistency. If you are in a hurry, ready-prepared canned garbanzo beans may be used. Much appreciated in North Africa, garbanzo beans were introduced to the island of Malta by Moorish invaders.

The garbanzo beans, slices of tuna, and tomato salad are made even more delicious by the addition of olive oil, although Maltese cooks often use corn oil as olive trees are scarce on the island, and there is only one brand of local olive oil.

The tomato salad is served on toasted slices of Maltese bread called *hobza*, giving a rather more elaborate version of a Maltese favorite *hobz biz-zejt* ("bread with oil") eaten as a snack or with a drink in bars.

Garnish the dish with arugola leaves and drizzle with olive oil.

To make the garbanzo purée, first soak the beans overnight in water. The next day, rinse them and cook for 2 hours (or until soft) in a pan of boiling water. Drain them, reserving some of the cooking water, and blend them in a food processor with a little of the liquid.

Peel and chop the garlic together with the anchovies and the parsley. Add them to the puréed garbanzo beans. Add a little oil, salt, and pepper. Mix well and set aside in a cool place.

For the tomato salad, peel the tomatoes and cut into small dice. Chop the basil and parsley. Peel and chop the garlic and red onion. Chop the capers. Place all these ingredients in a bowl.

Garbanzo Purée

Pour a little olive oil over the salad and season with salt and pepper. Mix well with a spoon.

Toast the slices of bread and top them with the tomato salad.

Slice the tuna into thin pieces. Arrange 2 or 3 slices on one side of each plate, a piece of toast with tomato salad in the center, and some garbanzo purée on the other side. Drizzle with olive oil and serve cold.

Soups

Aljotta

Preparation time:	*35 minutes*
Cooking time:	*50 minutes*
Difficulty:	★★

Serves 4

4 lb/2 kg	fresh fish fillets (scorpion fish, red snapper, sea bass)
2	carrots
2	red or yellow onions
3	bay leaves

2 tbsp/30 ml	olive oil
4	tomatoes
5 or 6 leaves	fresh basil
2 or 3 sprigs	fresh marjoram
5 or 6 leaves	fresh mint
½ cup/100 g	long grain rice
	salt and pepper

Malta's numerous delicious fish soups draw on the abundance of fish in the island's waters in summertime. Not dissimilar to the southern French soup bouillabaisse, the popular *aljotta* takes its name from the Italian word for garlic, *aglio*, which is an important feature of this recipe. Unlike bouillabaisse, *aljotta* never includes shellfish.

Aljotta is a traditional recipe designed to use up any surplus fish, combining them with tomatoes, red bell peppers, marjoram and other herbs, garlic, and some rice to give body. Michael Cauchi prefers to use onions rather than garlic in his version of this dish because they give a better texture. In the past, this tasty soup was prepared in an earthenware pot and cooked very slowly over a *kenur*, a small stone oven filled with hot embers.

A number of different fish are used for this recipe depending on the catch: scorpion fish, mullet, sea bass, or rock fish. They can be cooked whole, including the heads and bones. The flesh is removed when the fish is cooked and the bones returned to the bouillon that should continue to simmer until it has reduced by half, leaving a well-flavored basis for the soup. To save time, you can use ready-filleted fish that require less cooking time.

Carrots, bay leaves, and onion (red or yellow) are used to flavor the bouillon. Celery can also be added.

The last stage of preparation, cooking the rice in the soup, will take about 20 minutes. Be careful that the rice does not dry out, adding water as necessary until it is soft. After this, the pieces of fish are returned to the soup, which is served very hot.

Place the fish fillets in a saucepan with 1 chopped carrot, 1 sliced onion, and the bay leaves. Season with pepper and cover with water. Bring to the boil and simmer for 3–4 minutes.

Skim the bouillon and lift out the fish with a spatula. Set the fish aside on a plate and reserve the bouillon.

In another saucepan, lightly brown 1 sliced onion mixed with 1 grated carrot, in the oil. Add the skinned, chopped tomatoes and stir vigorously over the heat to obtain a smooth sauce.

Strain the fish bouillon. Add the roughly chopped basil, marjoram, and mint to the vegetable mixture, followed by the bouillon. Bring everything to the boil.

Once the mixture is boiling, add the rice with some salt and pepper. Allow to cook for 20 minutes.

When the rice is soft, break the fish fillets into large pieces and return them to the soup. Check the seasoning and serve immediately.

Tal-Grottli

Preparation time: *40 minutes*
Cooking time: *40 minutes*
Difficulty: ★★

Serves 4

4 sticks	celery
1	carrot
1	onion
12	small rock crabs
4 cloves	garlic
2 tbsp/30 ml	wild fennel tops
7 tbsp/100 ml	olive oil
2 tbsp/40 ml	tomato concentrate
4 or 5 sprigs	parsley
2 small glasses	Maltese anisette
	salt and pepper

A nourishing and delicious soup featuring rock crabs, *soppa tal-grottli* is traditionally a poor person's dish in Malta. Today, celebrated Maltese chefs often serve this type of recipe as an introduction to the island's authentic, traditional cuisine. It is hard to believe that, barely a decade ago, such delicacies were available only in modest village bars, or for family meals at home. Nowadays, cookery programs on television and radio, and magazine and newspaper articles, are furthering the chefs' efforts to rediscover and promote these dishes.

The name of this soup comes from the Maltese word *grottli*, small rock crabs with a very tough, hairy shell and large claws. They contain only a small amount of flesh and so are usually used for soups. They are cooked whole, in their shells, giving a rich flavor to the cooking liquid. The Maltese catch the crabs on the beaches at night, using a kind of fork.

It is important to strain this soup very carefully after cooking the crabs—either into a bowl or directly into the pan containing the tomato sauce—in order to remove all the pieces of crab shell and the remains of the vegetables. To get the most from the crabmeat and the other flavors, press the ingredients through the sieve with a pestle.

Unless very ripe, well-flavored fresh tomatoes are available, tomato concentrate added to fried garlic will be ideal for this recipe. Do not add the anisette until the last minute, otherwise it will evaporate and its flavor will be lost.

Cut up the celery stems and roughly chop the leaves. Peel and chop the carrot and slice the onion.

Put the crabs in a large saucepan, cover with water, and add the prepared vegetables. Season with salt and pepper. Bring to the boil and cook for 30 minutes.

Transfer the vegetables and crabs to a large plate. Remove the crab claws and set aside.

Bisque

Tip the vegetables and crabs into the bowl of a food processor and mix gradually until a greenish-colored bisque is obtained.

Pass the bisque mixture carefully through a fine mesh sieve, into a bowl or pan.

In another pan, fry the chopped garlic and fennel plumes in the oil. Add the tomato concentrate and chopped parsley. Pour in the sieved bisque and the anisette. Reheat. Serve with a dribble of olive oil and garnished with parsley and the crab claws.

Cold Cream of Almonds

Preparation time:	*45 minutes*
Steeping time for vegetables and almonds:	*8 hours*
Difficulty:	★

Serves 4

2	scallions (spring onions)
1	onion
1 lb/500 g	ripe Mallorcan tomatoes
2	Mallorcan green bell peppers
1 cup/150 g	blanched Mallorcan almonds
1 tsp/5 g	paprika
3½ tbsp/50 ml	sherry vinegar
4/5 cup/200 ml	extra-virgin olive oil
	salt

Trampó is one of the favorite dishes eaten by country people on the Balearic Islands. The classic version consists simply of a refreshing summer salad of bell peppers, tomatoes, onions, and olives, dressed with good quality olive oil and vinegar. Some chefs serve it as an accompaniment to baked fish. Oscar Martínez Plaza has taken this classic recipe and created a marvelous new dish by mixing the ingredients with almond milk. A garnish of diced vegetables remains, however, to remind us of the dish's origins.

Oscar Martínez Plaza uses typical Balearic vegetables for this recipe. Mallorca, the largest of the islands, is famous for its vegetable produce. Since the island is not large, the vegetables are still very fresh when they reach the village markets or the main covered market in Palma, the Mercat Olivar.

The main vegetable crop on Mallorca is tomatoes, grown over an area of more than 2,500 acres/1,000 hectares. The tomatoes are often tied into bunches and sun-dried by hanging against the walls of the houses. Tomatoes dried in this way are known as *tomàtigues de ramellet* in Catalan, or *tomates de ramillete* in Castilian.

The idea of combining *trampó* with almonds is not so surprising, since almonds grow abundantly on the Balearic Islands. The Arabs who colonized these islands between the 8th and the 13th centuries introduced and cultivated both almonds and figs. Mallorcan almonds, while irregular in size and so not considered to be of the finest quality, have a fine flavor. Mixed with water and the vegetables, they should be allowed to soak for a long time in order to rehydrate, becoming juicy and easier to mix. The resulting soup is both tasty and elegant.

Wash the vegetables. Chop the scallions, peel and chop the onions, and cut the tomatoes into quarters. Cut open the peppers, remove the seeds, and roughly chop (reserve a half of each type of vegetable for the garnish).

Mix all the vegetables in a bowl. Add the almonds and the paprika, reserving a few almonds for the garnish. Cover with water and leave to soak for 8 hours. Drain.

Tip the ingredients into a food processor and blend until creamy.

with Trampó

Add salt, the vinegar, and $^{2}/_{3}$ cup of olive oil. Blend again.

Sieve the creamed vegetables into a bowl.

Cut the reserved halves of tomato, onion, green pepper, and scallion into small dice. Season with salt and $3^{1}/_{2}$ tbsp of olive oil. Pour the soup into soup bowls, garnishing it with a few almonds surrounded by a circle of vegetable dice.

Kusksu

Preparation time: *25 minutes*
Cooking time: *1 hour 10 minutes*
Difficulty: ★

Serves 4

9 oz/250 g	fresh fava beans (broad beans)
²/₃ cup/100 g	fresh peas
2	medium onions
3 cloves	garlic

3½ tbsp/50 ml	corn oil
½ stick/50 g	butter
5 tbsp/100 g	tomato concentrate
1	bay leaf
4 cups/1 liter	beef bouillon
9 oz/250 g	*kusksu* pasta
	parmesan
	salt and pepper

For many centuries, it has been traditional on Malta to serve *kusksu* at Easter, the season when fava beans and peas are green and tender. The name of this soup sounds like "couscous" and although the recipe is very different from the famous North African dish, the word may be derived from the presence of the small, seed-like pieces of pasta, which are similar to coarse couscous grains.

Soup is a popular item on Maltese menus. Light fish soups are eaten in the summer, while in the winter, thick soups made with local vegetables are common. There are many small market gardens on Malta, growing a wide range of vegetables that are offered for sale, freshly picked, in small village shops and on stalls at the big market on Merchants Street in Valletta.

The pasta used in this traditional soup is called *pasta ta'l kusksu* in Maltese. It consists of very small, multifaceted balls that are made by just one producer on Malta. Used solely in the preparation of *kusksu*, the pasta is only manufactured around Easter time. With such a small level of production, like several other Maltese specialties, it is not exported. A variety of similar types of pasta can be found in Italy, however, including *acini di pepe* ("pepper seeds").

It will be noted that, in this recipe, Johann Chetcuti uses a mixture of corn oil and butter to brown the garlic and onions. This is because, unlike their Mediterranean neighbors, the Maltese do not cook exclusively with olive oil. Olive trees are relatively scarce on the island and olive oil is not produced on a commercial scale.

The soup is delicious served with grated or shaved parmesan. To make the soup even richer, some Maltese add a few spoonfuls of ricotta, or a few of the tiny goat cheeses produced on the island of Gozo.

Shell the fava beans and peas. Peel and chop the onions and the garlic, and brown them for 5 minutes in a large pan in a mixture of corn oil and butter.

Add the tomato concentrate to the pan. Cook for 3 minutes, stirring all the time.

Add the bay leaf and then the bouillon. Bring it to the boil.

When the bouillon has come to the boil, add the beans and peas. Simmer for 30 minutes.

Now add the pasta. Cook for 20 minutes until it is soft. Season to taste with salt and pepper.

When ready to serve, add the grated parmesan and mix well. Garnish with shavings of parmesan.

Bastia Fish

Preparation time: *35 minutes*
Cooking time: *1 hour 45 minutes*
Difficulty: ★

Serves 4

2 lb/800 g	small lobsters (langoustines, Dublin Bay prawns, Florida lobsterettes etc.)
1	spider crab
3 lb/1.5 kg	mixed fish for soup (gray mullet, whiting, conger eel etc.)
7 tbsp/100 ml	white wine
4 oz/100 g	fresh scallions (spring onions)
2 lb/800 g	mussels
1/4	fennel bulb
1/2 bunch	parsley
4 cloves	garlic
1/4 cup/60 ml	olive oil
1 tbsp/20 g	tomato concentrate
1 pinch/1 g	saffron powder
1 lb/400 g	fish fillets (sea bass, dentex, rock salmon, dog fish etc.)
2 1/2 tbsp/40 ml	light cream
1 stalk	*nepita* (wild mint)
	salt and pepper

Typical of the Corsican coastal areas, this traditional fisherman's soup is similar to the southern French bouillabaisse. A meal in itself, it is made with whatever fish and seafood are available. Although it is easy to prepare, it requires a long cooking time.

This Corsican specialty comes from the magnificent city of Bastia, overlooking the Mediterranean. Fishing in Corsica is still carried out in small boats equipped with lines and nets, with trawlers rarely being used. The boats return to port with many different types of high quality fish for the market stalls, including John Dory, gurnard, sea bass, red scorpion fish, mullet, and dog fish. In addition to these there are crawfish, caught in pots woven from myrtle or willow branches.

Corsicans have traditionally used small crabs and rock fish to give extra flavor to this soup. Cooked in their shells together with olive oil, garlic, onion, fennel, and tomatoes, the crabs are then liquidized with the bouillon, and strained through a fine sieve, giving a deliciously concentrated aroma. Vincent Tabarani recommends using a spider crab in this recipe. This spiny-shelled crab with delicate legs and long claws is considered by some to be the most delicately flavored of all the crustacea. It is generally poached in a court bouillon (a light, acidic stock used for quick-cooking seafood) and eaten cold.

This soup gains its extra subtlety from the addition of saffron, the most expensive spice in the world and one with its unique taste. It should be used very sparingly, as too much will give a bitter flavor.

Nepita, the peppery-tasting wild mint native to the Corsican *maquis*, is a reminder of this soup's proud origins.

Remove the flesh from the lobsters and set aside, with the heads and shells. Cut up the spider crab. Reserve the juices from the head. Cut the fish for the soup into large chunks.

Pour the white wine into a large saucepan and add half a chopped scallion. Add the cleaned mussels and cook for a few minutes until they have opened. Remove the mussels from their shells. Reserve the cooking liquid.

Wash and chop the fennel, parsley, and the remaining onions. Crush the garlic. Brown these ingredients in a saucepan with the olive oil.

Soup

Add the tomato concentrate, followed by the langoustine shells and heads, the fish for the soup, and the pieces of spider crab. Crush these with a wooden spoon during cooking to release the flavors.

Pour the liquid used for cooking the mussels, and the juices from the head of the spider crab, into the fish mixture. Cover with water, and cook for 1–1½ hours. Season with salt and pepper. Strain the bouillon.

Sprinkle the saffron into the bouillon. Add the mussels, the fish fillets cut into chunks, and the flesh of the lobsters. Cook for about 2 minutes. Pour the cream into the soup, add the chopped nepita, *and serve.*

Menorcan Crawfish

Preparation time: *45 minutes*
Cooking time: *45 minutes*
Difficulty: ★★

Serves 4

1	Menorcan crawfish weighing 3 lb/1.5 kg
4/5 cup/200 ml	olive oil
4/5 cup/200 ml	brandy
1	onion
1 clove	garlic
1	tomato
10 cups/2.5 liters	fish bouillon

For the *majado*:

1 cup/150 g	blanched almonds
	olive oil for frying
	crawfish "coral"
2 cloves	garlic
1 sprig	parsley
1 sprig	fresh thyme
2 or 3 slices	bread
7 tbsp/100 ml	Mallorcan herb liqueur

For the toast:

8 slices	stale bread
1 clove	garlic
1/4 cup/50 g	red pork fat

The small island of Menorca is famous for its crawfish soup. Known all over the island, *caldereta de langosta*, as it is called locally, has put the northern bay of Cala Fornells firmly on the culinary map.

Menorcan fishermen catch the crawfish in woven pots placed on the sea floor. The crawfish feeding grounds lie off the rocky shores of the Balearic Islands; here they find the shellfish that give such a delicate flavor to their meat. Strict rules are imposed to protect this valuable natural resource, with fishing restricted to the period from May to September. Any crawfish that are smaller than 8 inches/19 cm in length must be returned to the sea.

To prepare the live crawfish, place it on a chopping board and hold its head down firmly with a cloth. With the other hand, cut through the neck with a cleaver. Empty the orange parts found within the head (the "coral") into a bowl. Chop the head open in order to get at the remaining coral. This will be used to bind, color, and flavor the *majado*, a pounded or mixed paste used to thicken the bouillon.

The bouillon is generally made from rock fish (whole or scrap pieces), lightly browned with tomatoes, onions, and garlic and then covered with water. This mixture is brought to the boil and then simmered. Alternatively, a good quality fish bouillon cube can be used, adding the vegetables and the crawfish shells.

The *majado* used to give body to the bouillon is based on almonds and flavored with a Mallorcan liqueur made of local herbs. This aniseed-flavored digestive has a beautiful green color, perfumed with rosemary, marjoram, lime flowers, chamomile, fennel, and mint. A good-quality Provençal pastis can be substituted if necessary.

Fry the blanched almonds in the olive oil and set aside. Holding the crawfish firmly on a chopping board, sever the head and empty the coral into a bowl for use later. Blanch the crawfish tail in boiling water and then remove the shell.

Heat 4/5 cup of olive oil in a pan. Add the pieces of crawfish head and brown them. Pour over the brandy and flambé it, shaking the pan. Continue for 2–3 minutes until the flames have died down.

Add 1 onion, 1 garlic clove, and 1 tomato to the fish bouillon, bring it the boil and simmer for 10 minutes. Pour the bouillon over the pan containing the pieces of crawfish. Bring it to the boil again and cook for 15 minutes.

Soup

For the majado, *using a mortar, pound together the garlic, parsley, thyme, cubes of bread fried in oil (keep a few to garnish), the fried almonds, and the herb liqueur. Gradually add the crawfish coral, grinding the ingredients until a smooth paste has been obtained.*

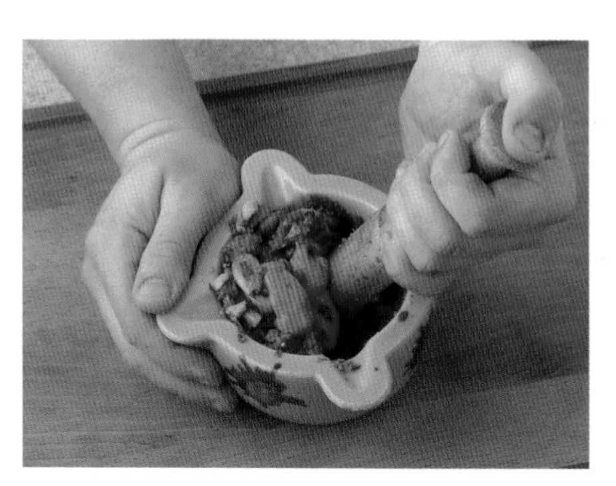

Leaving the bouillon on a low heat, add the majado *and mix it in to thicken the liquid. Turn up the heat for a few minutes.*

Toast the slices of bread, rub them with a garlic clove, then spread with red pork fat. Pour the soup into the bowls and place a lump of crawfish head and some of the meat from the tail in the center. Garnish with cubes of fried bread and herbs. Eat with the pieces of toasted bread.

Sopes Escaldades

Preparation time:	*30 minutes*
Cooking time:	*3 hours 20 minutes*
Difficulty:	★★

Serves 4

For the soup:

1	red bell pepper
1	green bell pepper
3	Mallorcan tomatoes
1	onion
2 cloves	garlic
½	green cabbage
4 oz/100 g	Swiss chard
4 oz/100 g	spinach
1 bunch	flat-leaf parsley

1 tbsp/15 g	paprika
½ cup/100 g	red pork fat
4 cups/1 liter	light bouillon
4 oz/100 g	country bread

For the meat:

2 cups/500 g	shortening
1 lb/400 g	slab of bacon
3 cloves	garlic
2 or 3 sprigs	fresh thyme
1	*sobrasada* (Mallorcan pork sausage)
1	*butifarron* (Mallorcan blood pudding)
4 tsp/20 ml	olive oil

Pigs have been reared on the Balearic Islands since ancient times. A pig festival is celebrated in Matançes every December. The best cuts and offal are eaten fried, while the remaining parts of the animal are turned into sausages (*sobrasadas*) and puddings such as *butifarron* and *camaiot*. These are used in many delicious dishes including the Matançes specialty, *sopes escaldades*.

Black and hairy rather than pink, the local pigs roam free in the woods and olive groves. Depending on the time of year, they feed on acorns, figs, carobs, or olives, a diet that gives the meat its justly famed flavor. Species of pink pig have been introduced to the islands, where they are now widespread, but their meat is less prized.

The soil of the Balearic Islands favors market gardening and a vast choice of vegetables is sold in the markets. For this recipe, bell peppers, garlic, onions, and tomatoes are browned in red pork fat. Known locally as *manteca roja*, the fat is obtained by cooking some pork in a bouillon. The layer of fat that forms on the surface is skimmed off and seasoned with spices. Similar in texture to shortening, it is orange in color.

Sobrasada and *butifarron* are made entirely from pig meat and offal, and simply oven-baked. *Sobrasada* is a dry brownish-red sausage made from a mixture of ground pork meat and fat to which paprika, salt, pepper, and spices are added. It is generally sliced, the soft interior being served on bread. It can also be cooked, as here. *Sobrasada de Mallorca de cerdo negro*, made from the meat of the black pig, is considered to be the best of these sausages. *Butifarron*, a gray-colored pudding, is made of the boiled rind and head of the pig, together with the meat and blood, all flavored with spices.

To make the soup, remove the seeds from the green and red bell peppers and chop them and the tomatoes into small dice. Chop the onion and garlic. Slice the cabbage, Swiss chard, spinach, and parsley.

Brown the garlic, peppers, tomatoes, onion, and paprika in the red fat. Mix for a few moments over the heat, and then add the light bouillon. Bring to the boil, and cook for 10 minutes.

Add the sliced cabbage, Swiss chard, spinach, and parsley to the bouillon. Mix for 3–4 minutes over the heat.

from Matançes

Remove the lightly poached vegetables from the liquid with a spatula and put them on a plate. Reserve the bouillon.

To prepare the meat, arrange pieces of shortening in an ovenproof dish. Add the bacon, the garlic cloves, still in their skins but cut into halves, and the thyme. Cover with waxed or silicone paper and cook in a cool oven (250 °F/120 °C) for 2½–3 hours.

Cut the sobrasada *and the* butifarron *into chunks and fry them in a little oil. Arrange the toasted sliced bread in the soup bowls and cover them with the vegetables. Place the pieces of* butifarron, sobrasada, *and bacon around the toast and pour the bouillon over the top.*

Xinochondro

Preparation time: *30 minutes*
Cooking time: *1 hours 55 minutes*
Difficulty: ★

Serves 4

1³/₄ lb/800 g	leg of goat
1	carrot
1 stick	celery
¹/₂	zucchini
1 sprig	thyme
1	bay leaf

3 oz/80 g	*xinochondro*
¹/₃ cup/80 ml	olive oil
	juice of ¹/₂ lemon
11 oz/300 g	tomatoes
	salt and pepper
4 tsp/20 g	yogurt
4	fresh mint leaves

Xinochondro soup with goat meat is a dish prepared in many Cretan villages. For centuries, mutton and goat were the favorite meats eaten on the island. The local goats are allowed to range freely over the mountain pastures, which abound in aromatic grasses and herbs. As a result, their meat is healthy, lean, and full of flavor.

While the goat meat is stewing, be sure to skim the froth regularly with a spatula as it rises to the surface of the pot. Set a bowl full of cold water near the cooking pan. Each time you skim the meat, dip the spatula in the water to clean it, leaving behind the scum. If the meat is of good quality, this will be white rather than a suspect brown.

If goat meat is unobtainable, it is possible to make this recipe with pork, but the result will be a greasier dish. Since the soup itself is fairly substantial, some people eat it on its own without meat.

The piquant taste of *xinochondro* gives this soup its unique flavor. To make your own, as the Cretans do, place 2¹/₂ pints of sheep or goat's milk in a bowl and leave it for 3 or 4 days at room temperature until it curdles. Then boil it with 1 lb of cracked wheat and some salt. When the mixture is thick and smooth, leave it to cool and then break it up with a spoon. Leave it to dry in the sun or in a low oven.

Generally made at the end of August, *xinochondro* can be eaten immediately, but will remain fresh for several months. It forms into small lumps that can be crumbled when used in the soup.

In the villages of Crete, the soup is served in bowls accompanied by a plate of large pieces of meat. For this recipe Michalis Markakis suggests a less rustic presentation, the meat being cut into small pieces and mixed into the soup.

Remove the fat and gristle from the leg of goat meat. Cut the meat into cubes.

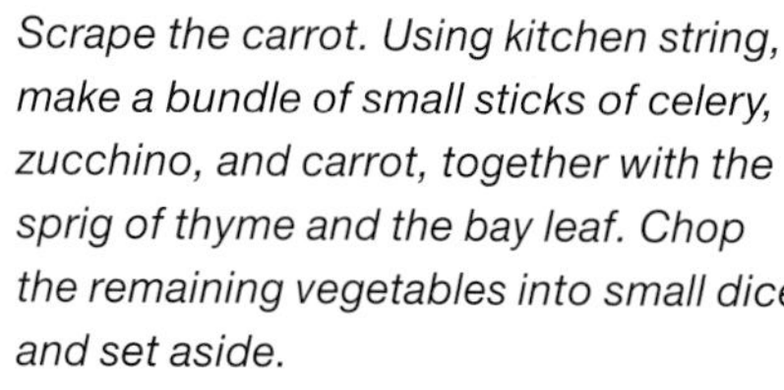

Scrape the carrot. Using kitchen string, make a bundle of small sticks of celery, zucchino, and carrot, together with the sprig of thyme and the bay leaf. Chop the remaining vegetables into small dice and set aside.

Place the goat meat in a large pot. Fill with cold water. Bring to the boil, then reduce the heat, skim, and add the bundle of vegetables and herbs. Simmer for 1 hour 40 minutes, skimming off the froth at intervals.

Soup

When the meat is cooked, remove it from the pot. Now add the crumbled xinochondro *to the cooking liquid.*

Add the olive oil, the lemon juice, and the chopped tomatoes. Season with salt and pepper.

Lastly, add the diced vegetables. Bring the soup back to the boil and simmer for 15 minutes. Serve in bowls with the meat. Top with a spoonful of yogurt and a fresh mint leaf.

St Lucy's

Preparation time:	*40 minutes*
Cooking time:	*2 hours 10 minutes*
Soaking time for the wheat:	*72 hours*
Soaking time for the garbanzo and navy beans:	*12 hours*
Difficulty:	★

Serves 4

1 cup/200 g	whole wheat grains
⅓ cup/50 g	garbanzo beans (chickpeas)
¼ cup/50 g	dry navy (haricot) beans

1½ lb/700 g	wild herbs and leaves (or wild chicory, Swiss chard, tarragon etc.)
2 cloves	garlic
1	onion
2 tbsp/30 ml	olive oil
1 oz/25 g	celery
2 oz/50 g	carrot
	salt

For the bouquet garni:

1 sprig	thyme
1 sprig	rosemary
2	marjoram leaves
1	bay leaf

To accompany:

	garlic toast

St Lucy is the patron saint of the magnificent city of Siracusa on Sicily, where she is commemorated with an annual festival. During the city's catastrophic famine of 1600, the inhabitants prayed to St Lucy for help, after which she is said to have caused boats full of wheat to arrive in the port. The starving people rushed to take the precious cargo, still damp with seawater. From it they made a soup flavored with the leaves of wild plants.

A very popular dish in Siracusa, this filling specialty is typically eaten in wintertime. Wheat has been cultivated on Sicily since Antiquity, for baking flour and durum wheat flour (used to make pasta). Sicily became known as the "granary of the Roman Empire" when the Romans converted much of the land there to the cultivation of wheat. Even today, there are villages where Ceres, the Roman goddess of agriculture, continues to be venerated. In preparing this soup, it is important to soak the wheat for a full 72 hours so that the grains can swell up and cook thoroughly.

This is a very simple soup to cook. Garbanzo and navy beans, later additions to the original recipe, make the soup even more nourishing.

The wild herbs and edible leaves are an essential feature of this rustic soup, and are much used in Sicilian cooking. They can be replaced, as they are here, by young Swiss chard and spinach leaves, wild chicory, and tarragon. Tarragon, a strongly aromatic herb, that originally came from Central Asia, adds a slight hint of aniseed and pepper to the dish.

Soak the wheat for 72 hours in a bowl of water. Soak the garbanzo and navy beans for 12 hours in separate bowls. Drain and cook the three items separately in simmering water, the wheat for 1 hour, the garbanzo beans for 1 hour, and the navy beans for 1 hour 30 minutes.

Wash the leaves. Cut up the chicory, Swiss chard, and tarragon. Blanch them in salted water for 3 minutes and drain. Now shred the leaves. Reserve the cooking liquid.

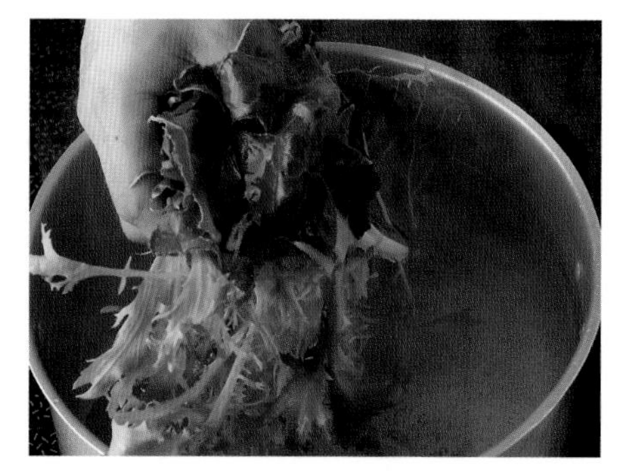

Brown the crushed garlic and chopped onion in olive oil. Add the celery and carrots, chopped into small dice. Cook for 5 minutes.

Wheat Soup

Tip the cooked wheat into the mixture. Add the shredded leaves. Cook for 5 minutes. Transfer the mixture into a large saucepan.

Pour the reserved liquid used for cooking the leaves over the mixture. Bring to the boil and simmer for 10 minutes.

Add the garbanzo and navy beans to the pan with the bouquet garni. Cook for a further 15 minutes. Season with salt. Serve the soup with bread rubbed with garlic and toasted.

Village

Preparation time: *45 minutes*
Cooking time: *1 hour 45 minutes*
Difficulty: ★

Serves 4

2 lb/1 kg	fresh fava beans (broad beans)
11 oz/300 g	potatoes
7 oz/200 g	young carrots
1	leek
7 oz/200 g	Swiss chard leaves
11 oz/300 g	scallions (spring onions)
4 oz/100 g	*nattarebulu* (dandelion leaves)
7 oz/200 g	pancetta
3½ tbsp/50 ml	olive oil
3 cloves	garlic
	salt and freshly ground pepper

For the garnish (optional):
fresh mint
fennel tops

Typical of Corsican cooking, this soup features many locally grown ingredients. Using vegetables from the garden, the soup varies from region to region, and from season to season. Vincent Tabarani was born in Ortiporiu in the heart of the Castagniccia region, from where he offers this ancestral recipe.

The fishermen, shepherds, and agricultural laborers of Corsica are deeply attached to their island. Herbs and other wild plants grow here in great abundance, and many have traditionally been eaten by the inhabitants. This recipe combines garlic, onions, leeks, and *nattarebulu* (dandelion), although *frisgiulla* (borage), with a taste similar to sorrel, could also be used.

Among the ingredients in this hearty vegetable-rich soup are fava beans. Much used in the Mediterranean area, the delicately flavored beans are grown in inland areas. Their relative, the garden pea, could be used in their place here, but fava beans are particularly nourishing. They can also be puréed or eaten as a salad. If young beans are used, there is no need to remove their outer skin. Choose small, firm pods that are bright green and without black marks.

Other vitamin-rich vegetables are used in the soup: carrots, leeks, and potatoes. Deliciously complementing the Swiss chard leaves, the vegetables are diced and cooked until they are tender but still firm. The Swiss chard is rich in potassium and magnesium, and gives a fresh flavor to the mixture. Spinach may also be used, instead of Swiss chard.

Finally, an essential ingredient of this delicious soup is a piece of fatty smoked bacon, *pancetta* or *buletta*, pork cheek or even a ham bone. In some villages on Corsica, the soup is made still more filling with the addition of pasta, rice, or slices of toasted bread.

Shell the fava beans. Chop the potatoes and carrots into dice. Slice the leek, Swiss chard leaves, scallions, and nattarebulu.

Cut the rind off the piece of pancetta and reserve. Cut the meat into small cubes.

Heat the olive oil in a saucepan and gently cook the pancetta without browning. Add the sliced scallions.

Soup

Add the sliced leek and sweat for a few minutes.

Cover the mixture with water. Add the pancetta rind and bring to the boil. Add the crushed garlic.

Add the rest of the vegetables. Season with salt and pepper. Simmer the soup for 1½ hours. Remove the pancetta rind and serve the soup in bowls.

Corsican

Preparation time: *40 minutes*
Cooking time: *2 hours 20 minutes*
Soaking time for dried beans: *12 hours*
Difficulty: ✭

Serves 4

1 cup/200 g	dried beans (red kidney and borlotti)
1 stick	celery

1	leek
3	carrots
11 oz/300 g	potatoes
1	onion
¼	green cabbage
1	ham bone
3 cloves	garlic
½ bunch	parsley
4 tsp/20 ml	olive oil
1 tbsp/20 g	tomato concentrate
5 oz/150 g	fresh tagliatelle
	salt and pepper

The ingredients of the homemade soups of garden vegetables eaten on Corsica vary according to the time of year. This very popular and filling dish is generally eaten in the evening. *Suppa corsa* is simple to prepare, retaining all the rustic goodness of Corsican home cooking.

In the remoter inland villages, soup was traditionally regarded as a meal in itself. The inhabitants of these areas were self-sufficient in food, and grew their vegetables in small plots arranged in terraces on the mountainsides, close to a stream and protected by low stone walls.

Vegetables commonly used for this soup are potatoes, celery, carrots, green cabbage, onions, and leeks. A ham bone is used to add strength and flavor. Since this can be quite salty, do not over-salt the soup when seasoning.

This is an easy recipe, but enough cooking time must be allowed to let the taste of the different ingredients penetrate fully into the beans. Introduced into Europe in the 16th century, these vitamin-rich beans are available in many varieties. We suggest you use borlotti beans, which are quite large, with dark red streaks and are particularly tasty. If they are bought dried, the beans should be soaked in water for 12 hours before cooking.

The ingredients of *suppa corsa* may be varied to cater for all tastes and seasons, producing different textures or flavors. In the recipe given here, Serge Fazzini has chosen to add some fresh tagliatelle. Some people prefer to blend the vegetables before eating, which you may or may not choose to do. However it is presented, this Corsican soup is an essential part of the island's heritage.

Soak the dried beans overnight. The next day, drain, rinse, then cook in clean water. The kidney beans must be fast-boiled for the first 10 minutes to destroy toxins, then continue to cook until soft (about 40 minutes).

Prepare the vegetables by cutting the celery into small dice and slicing the leek and carrots. Cut the potatoes into dice. Chop the onion and cabbage.

In a large saucepan, heat 7 pints/4 liters of water to which a pinch of salt and some pepper have been added. Place all the vegetables and the ham bone in the water and bring it to the boil. Simmer, uncovered, for about 1 hour.

Soup

In another pan, brown the garlic and chopped parsley in the olive oil. Add the tomato concentrate. Mix with a wooden spoon and then add to the soup.

Blend half of the beans in a food processor. Transfer this purée to the soup. Add the remaining whole beans. Cook the soup for about 30 minutes.

Remove the ham bone. Add the tagliatelle to the soup and cook for a further 10 minutes. Check the seasoning and serve the soup in bowls.

Zuppa di Fregola

Preparation time: *15 minutes*
Cooking time: *20 minutes*
Difficulty: ★

Serves 4

½ bunch	parsley
2 cloves	garlic
1	dried chile
1 oz/30 g	sun-dried tomatoes
2 lb/1 kg	medium clams
2 tbsp/30 ml	olive oil
1 cup/200 g	*fregola*
	salt and pepper

A Sardinian specialty often used in the preparation of soups, *fregola* is made of durum wheat flour and water. The tiny balls of flour are still made by hand, each ball being rolled between the fingers and then dried in the sun. This versatile, delicately flavored soup is a typically Sardinian recipe, featuring *fregola* and locally caught clams. If *fregola* are unavailable, use bulgur wheat, cracked wheat, or rice instead.

Local agricultural produce is the mainstay of Sardinian cooking, but there are also many seafood specialties. The dramatically beautiful coastline—all 833 miles/1,340 kilometers of it—abounds in fish and seafood, including the famous Alghero lobsters.

This recipe features delicious Mediterranean clams, identifiable by their thin, rounded shells and colors ranging from pale yellow to dark gray. Before cooking, be sure to soak them for a while in a bowl of water. This will help get rid of any sand inside the shells. Clams may also be eaten raw with a squeeze of lemon juice. If clams are unobtainable, substitute mussels or cockles.

Zuppa di fregola is a traditional fisherman's dish and very easily prepared. The distinctive flavor of parsley is an important element in the recipe. Available on the market stalls all year round, parsley is frequently used in Sardinian cooking. To give extra body to this soup, Amerigo Murgia suggests adding a chicken or beef bouillon cube.

Wash and chop the parsley. Peel and chop the garlic. Cut the chile and dried tomatoes into very fine slices.

Soak the clams in fresh water and then place them in a pan with a little water. Cook for about 5 minutes until they open. Strain off the cooking liquid and reserve.

Heat the olive oil in a pan and add the garlic and parsley. Mix and then add the sliced tomatoes and chile pepper. Cover with a little water and season with salt.

with Clams

Sprinkle the fregola *over the tomato and chile pepper mixture. Mix gently.*

Now add the reserved liquid used to cook the clams and stir.

Add the clams to the soup and cook for about 8 minutes. Serve in bowls.

Vegetarian Dishes

Shepherd's

Preparation time: *25 minutes*
Cooking time: *15 minutes*
Resting time for the batter: *1 hour*
Difficulty: ★

Serves 4

For the batter:

3½ cups/400 g	flour
½ envelope	dried yeast
2	eggs
1⅔ cups/400 ml	milk
1	soft ewe's- or goat's-milk cheese
	salt

1	lettuce
2 cups/500 ml	vegetable oil for frying

For the dressing:

1 tbsp/15 ml	balsamic vinegar
3 tbsp/45 ml	olive oil
	salt and pepper

Corsica's cuisine owes much to the island's strong pastoral tradition. The milk from Corsica's sheep and goats is used to make cheeses that are as renowned as its charcuterie and chestnuts.

Buglidicce are delicious fritters of soft, salty cheese. Originally a shepherd's dish, today this specialty is often eaten as a hot appetizer. Accompanied by a green salad, this easily made recipe makes an ideal light lunch.

Far from the pounding surf of the coast, the mountainous Niolo region rises to over 3,000 feet/1,000 meters above sea level, its slopes scattered with sheepfolds redolent of life in ancient Corsica. In this harsh, remote landscape, people lived virtually self-sufficient, fiercely independent lives for centuries. Their flocks were their only wealth. Inevitably, the shepherds were also cheese-makers.

Still made in the traditional way, from the milk of ewes and goats, Corsican cheeses are notable for their fine flavor. The fresh milk is strained through a cloth into a container. Rennet is added, from a dried kid's stomach. The cheese is turned 24 hours later, and salted on each of the following two days.

Eaten when still young and fresh, soft Corsican cheeses such as *brocciu* are ideal for making *buglidicce*. This delicious dish is a reminder to us all that the simple food of our ancestors can be every bit as good as today's elaborate cuisine.

To make the batter, place the flour, yeast, a pinch of salt, and the eggs in a bowl and mix.

Pour the milk into the flour mixture and beat with a whisk until a smooth paste is obtained.

Crumble the ewe's- or goat's-milk cheese.

Buglidicce

Add the cheese to the batter. Mix carefully with a wooden spoon. Leave to rest for one hour.

Wash the lettuce, discarding the outer leaves. To make the dressing, put some salt and pepper into a bowl. Pour in the balsamic vinegar and mix. Add the olive oil and beat with a fork.

Heat the frying oil in a pan. Form fritters from the batter mixture using two tablespoons, and carefully lower them into the oil. When golden brown, remove and drain on a piece of paper towel. Arrange the salad and fritters on the plates and pour over the dressing.

Shepherd's

Preparation time:	*1 hour*
Cooking time:	*40 minutes*
Difficulty:	★

Serves 4

For the batter:

2 cups/500 ml	milk
3	eggs
2¼ cups/250 g	flour
	salt and pepper

For the filling:

1 lb/500 g	spinach
1 tbsp/15 ml	olive oil
1 clove	garlic
1 lb/500 g	ricotta
4 oz/100 g	grated pecorino
3½ tbsp/50 ml	brandy
1 tsp/5 g	ground nutmeg
1	egg
	salt and pepper

For the tomato sauce:

½	onion
1 clove	garlic
2 tbsp/30 ml	olive oil
1 lb/500 g	tomatoes
½ bunch	basil
	salt and pepper

For the béchamel sauce:

2 cups/500 ml	milk
1½ sticks/150 g	butter
3 tbsp/50 g	flour
1 tsp/5 g	ground nutmeg
	salt and pepper

For the garnish: parsley

Lying off the tip of the boot-shaped Italian mainland, Sicily is an island whose strong pastoral tradition has had an important influence on the local cuisine. *Cannelloni alla pecoraia* is a very popular dish drawing on a number of locally produced ingredients. The cannelloni made here can be filled with different stuffings and eaten as an alternative to pasta. The delicious vegetarian stuffing used for this recipe features local cheese and spinach.

This is a substantial dish, and can be served either in small portions as an appetizer or as a main course. The cannelloni are easy to prepare, but ensure that the batter is perfectly smooth before it is used.

The main ingredient of the rich filling is ricotta. This soft cheese, made from the whey of goat's or ewe's milk, retains the shape of the container in which it is prepared. Mild and creamy, it makes a delicious addition to dressed salads, sauces, and pasta dishes. It's an important ingredient on Sicily, where guests arriving late are often greeted with assurances that they have arrived at just the right time, "like ricotta on pasta"! In the past, shepherds would sell this cheese on street stalls, in containers made of woven rushes. Today, it is readily available in food stores and supermarkets.

The ricotta is enlivened here with the flavors of grated pecorino and spinach. Originating in Persia, spinach is available on the market stalls in the spring and fall. To remove any bitterness from the leaves, it is a good idea to blanch them before use. Angelo La Spina adds a garlic clove and some olive oil when doing this. Choose regularly shaped, whole leaves free of any black spots. Wash them under running water rather than by soaking. Young Swiss chard leaves can be used as an alternative, when available.

For the batter, pour the milk into a bowl. Add the eggs with salt and pepper. Mix together. Gradually add the flour, beating the mixture continuously with a whisk until a runny batter is obtained.

Pour a little olive oil into a frying pan. Using a ladle, make pancakes with the batter.

For the filling, wash the spinach and put it in a saucepan with 1 tbsp of olive oil, a garlic clove, and two glasses of water. Blanch the spinach. Then chop it up and mix it with the ricotta, pecorino, brandy, nutmeg, salt, pepper, and an egg white.

Cannelloni

For the tomato sauce, brown the chopped onion and garlic in the olive oil. Add the chopped tomatoes and season with salt and pepper. Add the chopped basil. Cook the sauce over a gentle heat for 15–20 minutes.

For the béchamel, warm the milk and butter. Season with salt and pepper. Add some water to the flour to make a paste, and add it to the milk and butter when they come to the boil. Mix well and add the nutmeg. Fill each pancake with the stuffing and roll it up.

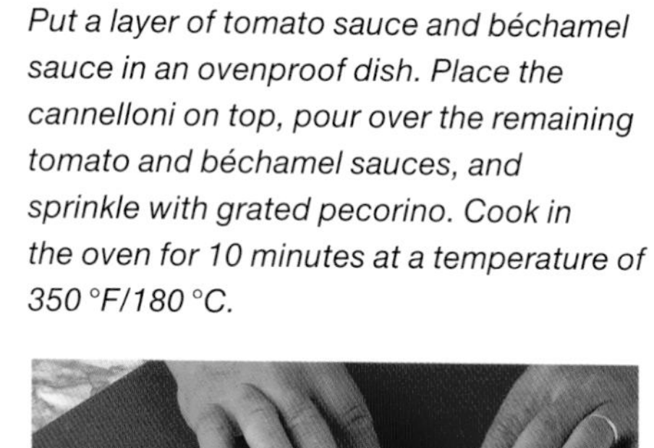

Put a layer of tomato sauce and béchamel sauce in an ovenproof dish. Place the cannelloni on top, pour over the remaining tomato and béchamel sauces, and sprinkle with grated pecorino. Cook in the oven for 10 minutes at a temperature of 350 °F/180 °C.

Souffléed Pancakes

Preparation time:	*30 minutes*
Cooking time:	*1 hour*
Refrigeration of batter:	*1 hour*
Difficulty:	★

Serves 4

For the batter:

2¼ cups/250 g	flour
3½ tbsp/50 ml	olive oil
5	eggs
	salt
2 cups/500 ml	Pietra beer

For the tomato coulis:

4	basil leaves
2 cloves	garlic
1	onion
1 sprig	*nepita* (wild mint)
2 tbsp/30 ml	olive oil
1 lb/500 g	tomatoes
	salt and pepper

For the filling:

1¼ lb/600 g	*brocciu* (Corsican cheese)
4	eggs
½ bunch	parsley
18	mint leaves
1	piece of shortening
or	
7 tbsp/100 ml	olive oil
	salt and freshly ground pepper

For the garnish:

	mint leaves

Bursting with typically Corsican flavors, these souffléed pancakes with *brocciu*, served with a tomato coulis, can be eaten as a hot appetizer. When creating this recipe, Vincent Tabarani was inspired by the famous *nicci*, traditional cookies made with chestnut flour and cooked on a griddle. This welcoming dish will be appreciated on any occasion.

As an ambassador for the *Cucina Corsa* (Corsican Cooking) Association, Vincent Tabarani is full of enthusiasm for his island's home-produced specialties. To give the pancakes an extra-light touch, he makes the batter with Pietra beer. Made in Furiani, at a brewery established about ten years ago, this highly characterful beer is flavored with herbs and chestnuts. Use any strong-flavored dark beer as a substitute, if Pietra is unavailable.

The pancakes make a substantial dish when filled with *brocciu*. This mild cheese has been made for generations on Corsica. Ricotta or *brousse* (from the Ardèche region of France) make good substitutes. It is advisable to place the filled pancakes on a sheet of baking parchment before browning them in the oven. This will make it easier to transfer them to the plates for serving.

A rich tomato coulis is frequently used in Corsican cooking. Here, the sauce is made from fresh tomatoes; however, traditional Corsican coulis takes the form of a thick, sun-dried paste, prepared in large quantities toward the end of the summer. The tomatoes are cut into pieces, and placed in a wooden tub with a hole at the bottom, closed with a cork. As the tomatoes ferment, they release a very acid liquid that is drawn off through the hole. The remaining flesh and pips are then drained in a cloth bag. The resulting tomato purée is spread on a wooden board to dry in the sun. When it darkens, it is put into earthenware pots and sealed with a thin layer of olive oil.

For the batter, put the flour into a bowl and add the olive oil, the eggs, and a pinch of salt. Mix with a wooden spoon.

Gradually add the beer to the mixture, stirring all the while. Beat with a fork to remove any lumps.

Strain the batter through a sieve, and refrigerate for 1 hour. Prepare the coulis by browning the chopped basil, garlic, onion, and nepita *in the olive oil. Add the diced tomatoes. Season with salt and pepper. Cook for 30 minutes and then blend in a food processor.*

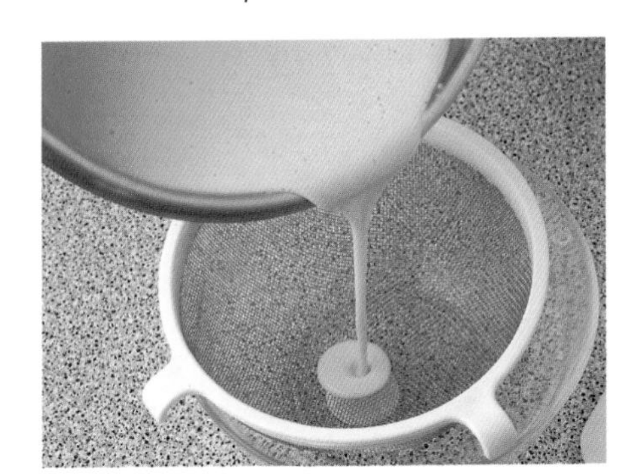

with Brocciu

Put the brocciu *and 4 egg yolks in a bowl. Season with salt and pepper and mix. Add the chopped parsley and mint. Beat the egg whites and a pinch of salt until stiff. Fold the whites into the filling mixture.*

Grease a pan with the shortening. Pour a ladleful of batter into the pan for each pancake. Cook on both sides. Heat the oven to a temperature of 350 °F/180 °C. Fill each pancake with 1 tbsp of the cheese mixture and fold it over in half.

Place the folded pancakes in an ovenproof dish and cook in the pre-heated oven for 8–10 minutes. When ready, arrange the pancakes on plates with the tomato coulis. Garnish with the mint leaves.

Culurgioni

Preparation time:	*1 hour*
Cooking time:	*1 hour*
Resting time for pasta:	*30 minutes*
Difficulty:	★★

Serves 4

For the pasta:

1 lb/500 g	flour
1	egg
½ tsp/pinch	saffron powder (optional)
	salt

For the filling:

1	onion
3 tbsp/45 ml	olive oil
4 cloves	garlic
1 bunch	fresh mint
1¼ lb/600 g	potatoes
3½ oz/100 g	grated pecorino
11 oz/300 g	*casu aceddu* (salty ewe's-milk cheese)

For the tomato sauce:

2 lb/1 kg	tomatoes
1	carrot
1 stick	celery
1 clove	garlic
1	onion
1	bay leaf
3	basil leaves
3 tbsp/45 ml	olive oil
	salt and pepper

For the garnish:

7 oz/200 g	grated pecorino
	basil leaves

Culurgioni are a delicious type of ravioli. A substantial dish, this popular specialty makes use of several typically Sardinian products. Requiring much dexterity and patience, the local cooks are highly skilled in making this stuffed pasta.

Also known as *culurzone*, *culurgioni* can be recognized by their characteristic shape. The ingredients used for the traditionally vegetarian stuffing can vary from household to household. The recipe given here by Amerigo Murgia is one of the classics, using cheeses, potatoes, mint, garlic, onion, and, of course, Mediterranean olive oil.

Sardinian pecorino cheese plays an important role in many of the island's traditional recipes, and is famous for its exceptional flavor. Flocks have grazed on the island of Sardinia for thousands of years. Today, there are more sheep than people. It has been estimated that one third of all the livestock in Italy today is to be found in Sardinia. Animal husbandry is the main source of income for the Sardinians, hence the island's many excellent cheeses.

In addition to pecorino, the filling used in this recipe calls for another typically Sardinian cheese, *casu aceddu*. A specialty of the Ogliastra region, it is similar to "blue" cheese. In the past, shepherds would eat it spread on potatoes baked in the embers of the fire. *Casu aceddu* can be eaten in its soft, freshly made state (similar to yogurt). It can also be salted and kept for about 12 months.

These simple, delicate Sardinian ravioli offer the pasta lover a veritable feast of concentrated flavors, complemented by those quintessential Mediterranean ingredients: garlic and, naturally, tomato sauce.

For the pasta, put the flour in a bowl and add the egg and saffron powder. Gradually add salted water. Work the mixture until an elastic pastry is obtained. Set this aside to rest for 30 minutes.

For the filling, brown the chopped onion in 2 tbsp of olive oil. Add the crushed garlic. Take the pan off the heat and add the chopped mint. Mix and set aside.

Cook the potatoes in boiling water for about 20 minutes. Peel them and then pass them through a potato-press into a bowl. Add the pecorino and casu aceddu. *Add the onion mixture and mix everything with your fingers. Add the remaining olive oil.*

Form the pastry into a ball and roll out with a rolling pin until it is very thin. Cut out circles.

Prepare the tomato sauce by cooking all the diced vegetables in olive oil, together with the herbs, for 30 minutes. Blend in a food processor and reserve. Using your fingers, make balls of the potato and herb filling, placing one on each round of pasta.

Fold the circles of pasta in half around the filling. Press lightly at one end, pinching the pasta into fan-like folds. Lower the culurgioni *into boiling water for about 4 minutes, remove, and arrange on plates with the tomato sauce. Garnish with grated pecorino and chopped basil.*

Dakos

Preparation time:	*35 minutes*
Cooking time:	*1 hour*
Resting time for dough:	*15 minutes*
Proving of dough in oven:	*15 minutes*
Difficulty:	★

Serves 4

2 lb/1 kg	regular wheat flour
7/8 cup/160 g	whole-wheat flour
7/8 cup/160 g	barley flour

2/3 oz/15 g	fresh baker's yeast
2/3 cup/150 ml	virgin olive oil
4	medium tomatoes
5 oz/150 g	feta cheese
	dried oregano
1 tsp/5 g	salt

Bread in all its forms has always been an important feature of the Cretan diet. A local proverb states that "foodstuffs are like separate threads: the stomach needs bread—the shuttle that weaves them together." The Greeks of Antiquity are known to have used a number of different varieties of flour to make their bread, which took innumerable forms, with a wide range of consistencies, shapes, and cooking methods.

Dakos or *paximadi* have been known on Crete since the Middle Ages. These rusk-like rolls are shaped into rings and baked once before being split into two and dried very slowly in a cool oven.

In the old days, country people prepared *dakos* only twice a year. The two-step baking process dried the loaves out so effectively that they would keep for several months. They were often eaten as a snack with some tomato and cheese (feta or *xinomyzithra*). Today, these crisp, healthy rolls are once again popular, making an excellent light snack.

Three types of flour—whole-wheat, regular wheat, and barley—are used for the dough. Many different types of cereals have been cultivated on Crete since Minoan times. Some village families still grind the flour at home with hand-turned millstones. The flour contains a lot of bran, giving the *dakos* a darker appearance.

When preparing these *dakos*, be generous with the oil, allowing them to become thoroughly impregnated. Not only does it give the bread a delicious taste, but also it will prevent the juice of the tomatoes from making the bread soggy. The rolls should be eaten while still crisp. Cretan virgin olive oil, obtained from small, purple olives, is dark green in color. Allowed to mature for at least a year, it will greatly enhance your *dakos*.

Combine the three flours in a bowl and add a little of the crumbled fresh yeast. (If using active dry yeast, follow maker's instructions.) Make a well in the middle and pour into it a scant cup of warm water. Add the salt and the rest of the yeast.

Knead the mixture with the tips of the fingers until a hard paste is obtained. Form this into a ball and leave it to rest for about 15 minutes at room temperature.

Divide the dough into large balls, each weighing about 11 oz/300 g. Shape the balls into rings and place them on an oiled baking sheet. Put them in a low oven to prove for 15 minutes, then raise the oven temperature to 400 °F/200 °C and bake them for 20 minutes.

Split each roll horizontally into two equal pieces. Reset the oven to the lower temperature (no more than 120 °F/50 °C) and return the rolls to the oven for about 40 minutes to dry out.

Arrange the rolls on plates and pour a generous amount of olive oil over them.

Blend the tomatoes in a food processor. Spread a spoonful of the puréed tomato over each roll. Sprinkle with crumbled feta cheese and a little oregano.
Serve cool.

Malloreddus

Preparation time:	*25 minutes*
Cooking time:	*20 minutes*
Difficulty:	★

Serves 4

7 oz/200 g	eggplant (aubergine)
1	red bell pepper
1	green bell pepper
1	yellow bell pepper
2	onions
5 tbsp/75 ml	olive oil
1 lb/500 g	*malloreddus* (pasta)
5	basil leaves
7 oz/200 g	grated ewe's-milk cheese (pecorino, or parmesan)
	salt and pepper

For the garnish:

basil leaves

Sardinian cooking is typically based on fresh local food and is, above all, copious and filling, with pasta every bit as important as bread. *Malloreddus*, also known since Antiquity as *gnocchetti sardi*, are a national specialty that perfectly expresses the richness of the island's ancient cuisine. Featuring sun-ripened Mediterranean produce, this vegetarian dish can be eaten both hot and, the next day, as a cold appetizer.

The Sardinian language is closely similar to Latin, and considered by linguists to be a Romance language in its own right rather than a dialect of Italian. The name *malloreddus* means "little calves" and refers to the elongated, horn-like shape of the pasta pieces.

Still made in the traditional way, the pasta consists of durum wheat flour, warm water, and salt, sometimes enriched with saffron, artichokes, or tomatoes. After prolonged kneading, it is divided into pieces of equal size and rolled out into fine strings. These are formed into the *malloreddus* using an ancient method that gives them their characteristic ridged appearance. They are available in specialist grocers and delicatessens, but if necessary can be replaced with penne.

This ideal family dish makes use of several typically Mediterranean vegetables, grown in abundance on the island. The sunny colors of the red, yellow, and green bell peppers will brighten up the table. Sardinian eggplants, grown in large quantities on the island's fertile plains, are celebrated for their excellent quality.

This dish is further enhanced by the deliciously perfumed local olive oil, and the delicate taste of basil. This herb, very frequently used in mainland Italian, Sardinian, and Sicilian cooking, is an ideal partner for use with tomatoes and pasta dishes.

Wash the vegetables and chop them all into small dice.

Pour the olive oil into a large pan. Heat it, and then add the diced vegetables. Cook for about 10 minutes. Season with salt and pepper.

Heat a large saucepan of water. When it boils, add salt and then the malloreddus. *Cook for about 9 minutes. Drain the pasta.*

Wash the basil leaves carefully and chop.

Add the malloreddus *to the vegetable mixture and mix carefully with a wooden spatula.*

Sprinkle the grated cheese and chopped basil over the pasta and serve. Garnish with basil leaves.

Palikaria

Preparation time: *15 minutes*
Cooking time: *30 minutes*
Soaking time for the dried vegetables: *overnight*
Difficulty: ★

Serves 4

7/8 cup/150 g	garbanzo beans (chickpeas)
3/4 cup/150 g	dried medium-sized white navy (haricot) beans
7/8 cup/150 g	dried fava beans (broad beans)
7/8 cup/150 g	husked durum wheat
3/4 cup/150 g	lentils
4	lemons
2/3 cup/150 ml	virgin olive oil
	salt and pepper

To garnish:
1 bunch dill

On January 5, the day before Epiphany, the country people of Crete would traditionally prepare a dish of boiled wheat and beans, flavored with olive oil, lemon, and herbs. After the family had eaten, the remains of the meal would be given to the domestic animals and birds as a sign of respect for all living creatures. Today, this energy-filled recipe is prepared all year round. It is often eaten on days when religious fasting is observed and meat and dairy products are off the menu. Known in eastern Crete as *palikaria*, it is also known in other parts of the island as *psarokolyva* and *mayeria*.

Historians believe that this dish takes its origin from the *panspermia* of ancient Greece—a dish offered to the gods in thanksgiving for a good harvest. It consisted of all the available seasonal grains and vegetables.

Navy, garbanzo, and fava beans, together with lentils, are among the most commonly used dried pulses on Crete. The locally grown fava beans have an attractive green color, while the garbanzo beans are orange-yellow. The resulting *palikaria* will thus present a delightful mix of colors—green, brown, and golden yellow.

All of the dried ingredients, with the exception of the lentils, need to be soaked before cooking. The ingredients for *palikaria* vary, but split peas should be avoided as they will become too soft, resulting in a mushy purée. When cooked, the pulses and wheat grains should be tender but retain their shape. Do not add salt to the cooking water or the pulses will remain hard. The wheat will need to be cooked for 30–45 minutes, depending on the brand.

This dish is better still if left to marinate for at least one night allowing the ingredients to fully absorb the flavors of the olive oil, lemon juice, and dill. The dill gives the dish a subtle, delicate hint of aniseed.

The night before, soak the garbanzo, navy, and fava beans and the durum wheat grains in cold water in four separate bowls.

The next day, drain the rehydrated beans and wheat. In four separate saucepans of boiling water, cook the fava beans, the lentils, the navy beans, and the garbanzo beans combined with the wheat, all for about 30 minutes.

Using a sieve, drain the pulses. Spread them on a cloth to dry.

Mix the pulses and wheat together in a large bowl.

Add the juice of the lemons, the olive oil, a pinch of salt, and a little pepper. Mix well.

Sprinkle the finely chopped dill over the dish, and serve well chilled.

Pane

Preparation time: *25 minutes*
Cooking time: *30 minutes*
Difficulty: ★

Serves 4

11 oz/300 g	*pane carasau* (sheets of durum wheat)
1	bouillon cube
4 oz/100 g	grated ewe's-milk cheese or parmesan
4 tbsp/60 ml	white wine vinegar
4	eggs

For the tomato sauce:

$1^{3}/_{4}$ lb/800 g	tomatoes
1	onion
1 stick	celery
1	carrot
3 tbsp/45 ml	olive oil
2 cloves	garlic
$^{1}/_{2}$ bunch	parsley
1	bay leaf
3	basil leaves
	salt and pepper

The Sardinians have a saying that their beautiful island was blessed by God—an earthly paradise providing a rich harvest for its fishermen and shepherds. Strongly influenced by the pastoral tradition, the island's cuisine is characterized by its simple, wholesome specialties. A good example is *pane fratau*, an ancient vegetarian dish.

This popular recipe is easy to make and requires good, fresh vegetables. *Pane carasau*, the thin sheets of durum wheat used in this dish, are a Sardinian specialty. Available from specialist grocers and delicatessens, it is also known as *carta di musica* ("music paper") because of its resemblance to the crisp parchment once used for sheet music.

The laborious task of making *pane carasau* is carried out by skilled bakers. The dough is kneaded several times before being placed in flat molds and baked twice. For this recipe, do not forget to dip the sheets of *pane carasau* in liquid before use to make them malleable. Sardinian shepherds generally prefer to use a bouillon of mutton or poultry for this.

Full of sun-drenched Mediterranean flavor, *pane fratau* is served with a tomato sauce sprinkled with pecorino, a ewe's-milk cheese.

Sardinia abounds in market gardens, and produces particularly well-flavored vegetables. The juicy Sardinian tomatoes are sold in the markets of Milan and Turin. They have a thin, smooth skin and very few seeds.

With the addition of poached eggs, this is a perfect dish for an informal meal with friends.

For the sauce, dice all the vegetables. Heat the olive oil and add the garlic and parsley. Add the diced tomato, onion, celery, carrot, together with the bay leaf. Cook for about 30 minutes. Season with salt and pepper. Add the chopped basil and blend the sauce in a food processor.

Break the pane carasau *into rough pieces. Dissolve the bouillon cube in a saucepan of hot water.*

Gently dip the pieces of pane carasau *into the bouillon to soften them. Place half of them on a serving dish, reserving the rest.*

Fratau

Pour half the tomato sauce over the pieces of pane carasau.

Sprinkle the dish with some of the grated cheese. Cover with the rest of the pane carasau *and then with another layer of tomato sauce and cheese.*

Heat 2 cups/500 ml of water. When boiling, add the vinegar and break the eggs into the liquid. Poach them for about 1 minute, then lift them gently with a spatula and place them on top of the dish of pane fratau.

Pasta Alla

Preparation time: *40 minutes*
Cooking time: *25 minutes*
Difficulty: ★

Serves 4

2	onions
2 cloves	garlic
1 stick	celery
1 bunch	parsley
1 bunch	basil
1¼ oz/30 g	sun-dried tomatoes
11 oz/300 g	tomatoes
3½ tbsp/50 ml	olive oil
1	small dried chile
1 tbsp/20 g	tomato concentrate
3½ tbsp/50 ml	white wine
1 lb/400 g	*bavette* (flat, slightly convex type of spaghetti about ⅛ inch/½ cm in width)
	salt

For the garnish:

cherry tomatoes (optional)
parsley
basil

A wide variety of pasta dishes are eaten on Sicily, at all occasions. An intrinsic part of the local culture, some of these delicious recipes have become classics, exemplifying all that is best in Sicilian cuisine. Notable specialties include *macaroni alla Norma*, made with eggplants, and *pasta con le sarde*, served with fresh sardines.

Pasta alla scarpara is a well-known summery vegetarian dish that originates from Caltagirone, the inland village where Angelo La Spina was born. He learned the recipe from the wife of the village cobbler (*scarparo*), who was fond of this easily made dish. It is important not to overcook the *bavette* (it should be served *al dente*: "with bite").

The invention of pasta is a claim proudly advanced—with numerous and varied historical proofs—by every region of Italy. The Sicilian theory credits the introduction of pasta to the island's Arab invaders in the 9th–11th centuries. Pasta was quickly adopted by the locals and became an essential part of the Sicilian diet. A work written in the 15th century mentions *maccheroni* being placed out in the August sun to dry.

Angelo La Spina uses *bavette*, a flat, slightly convex type of spaghetti, for this recipe. It is made equally well with tagliatelle or fettuccine.

This well-balanced and colorful dish is full of the flavors of the Mediterranean. Celery, a vegetable much employed in Sicilian cooking, combines deliciously with the tomatoes, onions, garlic, and basil. *Pasta alla scarpara* is quite simply *buonissima*.

Finely chop the onions. Crush the garlic cloves. Chop the celery, parsley, and basil. Cut up the sun-dried tomatoes. Peel the fresh tomatoes, remove the seeds, and mash them.

Brown the onions and garlic in the olive oil. Add the celery and cook for 5–6 minutes. Add the basil, parsley, and the dried tomatoes. Cook for a further 10 minutes. Season generously with salt and sprinkle on the ground chile.

Add the fresh tomato pulp to the mixture and mix with a wooden spatula. Add the tomato concentrate. Cook for about 5 minutes.

Scarpara

Pour over the white wine and mix in with a wooden spatula. Cook for another 5 minutes or so.

Heat a large saucepan full of salted water. Bring to the boil, add the bavette, *and cook for about 12 minutes, stirring occasionally with a fork. Drain the pasta.*

Transfer the pasta to the sauce and mix together over the heat. Serve the pasta alla scarpara, *garnished with cherry tomatoes, parsley, and basil.*

Pumpkin

Preparation time: *20 minutes*
Cooking time: *30 minutes*
Difficulty: ★

Serves 6

1 lb/450 g	pumpkin
7/8 cup/100 g	flour
7 tbsp/100 ml	olive oil
1 lb/450 g	shallots
7 tbsp/100 ml	wine vinegar

7 tbsp/100 ml	red wine
1	tomato
	Jamaican pepper (allspice)
1 pinch	cumin
2	bay leaves
1 sprig	rosemary
1 cup/100 g	black olives
	salt and freshly ground black pepper

In Greek, the word *stifado* ("stewed") usually describes a rich stew made with a dark sauce of shallots, spices, and wine. Cretans love to cook rabbit or hare in this way, but for a delicious vegetarian version, Michalis Markakis suggests using pumpkin in place of meat. Firm-textured chunks of pumpkin keep their shape well during cooking.

Unknown to the Greeks of Antiquity, pumpkins were a staple of the Amerindian diet for centuries, along with beans and maize. They were introduced to Europe from North America in the 16th century. This member of the gourd family is much eaten on Crete, appearing as an ingredient in stews, sweet tarts, and pies.

Michalis Markakis stresses the importance of very fresh pumpkin for this dish. Frozen pumpkin should not be used, as it tends to soften to a purée and give off too much liquid when cooking. Brown the pumpkin on all sides in the oil, using cooking tongs to turn and lift the cubes without breaking them.

For the shallot sauce, the Cretans simply cut up the tomatoes and crush them in the pan with the shallots, before or after the addition of other flavorings. Here, they are skinned first and blended in a food processor. The addition of the tomatoes will not affect the color of the sauce, which remains a rich orange-brown.

The powerful flavor of black olives enhances that of the pumpkin. Olive farms are found all over Crete, producing both olives and olive oil. When fully ripe, black olives are harvested and preserved in brine or dry-salted. Cretan olives can be so salty that they sometimes have to be blanched in water before use.

Cut the pumpkin into large pieces. Peel the chunks and remove the fibers and seeds. Cut the flesh into large cubes.

Cover the pieces of pumpkin with flour and brown them for about 10 minutes in half of the olive oil.

Peel the shallots. Brown them for 5 minutes in a sauté pan with the remaining oil, then deglaze with the vinegar and red wine. Add the puréed tomato.

Stifado

Add the herbs and spices: Jamaican pepper, cumin, bay leaves, rosemary, salt, and freshly ground pepper. Simmer the mixture for about 5 minutes until the shallots are soft.

Using cooking tongs, transfer the fried pieces of pumpkin to the shallot sauce.

Add the olives (blanch these first, if necessary). Leave the mixture to simmer for about 10 minutes over a medium heat. Serve with a garnish of your choice (hot, lightly buttered couscous makes an ideal accompaniment).

Turtera

Preparation time: *1 hour*
Cooking time: *2 hours 35 minutes*
Difficulty: ★★

Serves 4

1 piece	lamb bone (shank)
2	carrots
1 stick	celery
1	onion
3	bay leaves
½ stick/50 g	shortening

1 lb/500 g	ricotta
4 oz/100 g	3-month-old pecorino, grated
3½ tbsp/50 g	fresh marjoram
	salt and black pepper

For the *cavatini*:

2 cups/350 g	durum wheat flour
1¼ oz/30 g	dry pecorino, grated
1	egg
1 tbsp/15 ml	olive oil
	salt and black pepper

For Catholics, the rhythm of life on Sicily is marked by religious festivals, many of which are associated inextricably with traditional dishes of food. Easter is celebrated in fine style, and *turtera* (literally, pie) is traditionally associated with this time of year. A substantial pasta dish, *Turtera* is eaten as a hot appetizer.

Pasta, eaten with an almost infinite variety of sauces, is taken seriously on Sicily. The famous *cavatini* are made of durum wheat flour, egg, pecorino cheese, olive oil, salt, and pepper. Giuseppe Barone suggests that the name may be derived from the verb *cavare*, meaning to scrape or hollow out. The original *cavatini* had a grooved appearance, created by hand. They are available in Italian grocers, or instead use *cavatielli* or *garganelli*.

Full of rustic Sicilian flavors, the filling for these *turtera* also requires ricotta, a cheese made from the whey of cow's, ewe's, or goat's milk. If possible, do as the Sicilians do, and use the dry, stronger-tasting *ricotta dura* (hard ricotta) for pasta dishes, stuffings, and with vegetables.

Sicily is the setting for an episode of Homer's *Odyssey*, where it is described as a land of shepherds. The importance of the island's flocks of sheep is underlined by the famous passage in which Odysseus and his companions are taken prisoner by Polyphemus, one of the Cyclopes. The resourceful Greek hero manages to escape from his jailer by clinging to the underside of a sheep. Giuseppe Barone has made a study of the history of Sicilian food and believes that the Sicilians of Antiquity made a cheese very similar to the modern ricotta.

The flavors of this dish are enhanced by the use of the delicately scented herb marjoram. Similar in taste to mint or basil, it is much used in Mediterranean cooking.

For the pasta, mix the flour, salt, pepper, pecorino, egg, and olive oil in a bowl. Gradually add 7 tbsp/100 ml of water. Knead the mixture for about 15 minutes until it has formed into a dough. Leave it to rest for 5 minutes.

Cook the lamb bone with the roughly-chopped carrots, celery, and onion in a medium oven (350 °F/180 °C) for 30 minutes. Transfer these ingredients to a large saucepan filled with salted water and the bay leaves. Simmer for 2 hours. Strain the liquid and set aside.

Roll out the pasta dough on a flat surface to a thickness of ½ inch/1.5 cm. Cut it into strips. Cut these into small rectangles of equal size.

Place a rectangle on the upturned prongs of a fork, and press down as you roll it up, giving it a fluted appearance.

Bring the reserved bouillon to the boil and add the pasta. Cook for about 5 minutes. Remove it when cooked, reserving the bouillon.

Place half of the cooked pasta in a greased dish. Arrange some sliced ricotta on top. Season with pepper and then scatter on the grated pecorino. Add the marjoram and then a second layer of pasta. Pour the bouillon around the pasta and cook at 350 °F/180 °C for 30 minutes.

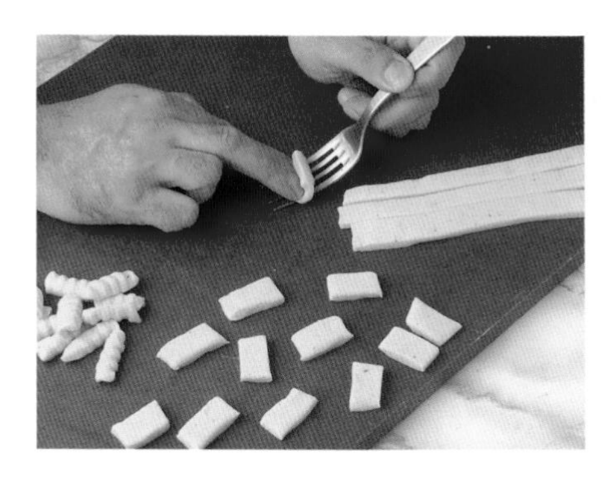

PARDU

Fish & Seafood

Arroz de Sepia

Preparation time: 1 hour
Cooking time: 50 minutes
Difficulty: ★★★

Serves 4

For the rice with cuttlefish ink:

1¾ lb/800 g	small cuttlefish
3	green bell peppers
7 tbsp/100 ml	olive oil
3	onions
4	tomatoes
1 pinch	paprika
7 oz/200 g	thin green beans
⅔ cup/100 g	fresh peas
1 cup/200 g	rice
4 tsp/20 ml	cuttlefish ink

For the fish bouillon:

heads & tails of 3	Mediterranean fish (gurnard, red snapper, sea bass)
7 tbsp/100 ml	olive oil
½	onion
1	leek
3 or 4	tomatoes
2 tbsp/30 g	paprika
1 sprig	thyme
2	bay leaves
3 or 4 sprigs	parsley

For the *picada*:
1 bulb garlic and ½ bunch flat-leaf parsley, ground together

For the garnish:

	a few green beans
½ envelope	cuttlefish ink
7 tbsp/100 ml	olive oil

Arroz de sepia, rice with cuttlefish, is one of most popular of the traditional recipes of the Balearic Islands. Enriched, Spanish style, with cuttlefish ink, it is generally served in the pan in which it is cooked.

Cuttlefish are used in many Iberian dishes. This saltwater mollusk thrives on the seabed near grassy coastlines. The cuttlefish has ten tentacles, two of which are very long and used to catch its prey. The body is a kind of flat, oval pocket covered in a grayish-mauve colored skin, and has small fins. Cuttlefish range from 4 to 16 inches/10 to 40 cm in length.

When threatened, cuttlefish disorientate and frighten their predators with a jet of black liquid. Spanish and Italian cooks were quick to appreciate the taste of this "ink," and it is used today in many famous dishes. Do not worry if the ink sacs of your cuttlefish are empty: it is possible to buy envelopes of cuttlefish ink.

Ideally, the bouillon in which the rice is to be cooked should be prepared with the heads and tails of small Mediterranean rock fish. A good fishmonger may be able to supply these (or the trimmings of other fish), but a good-quality ready-made fish bouillon could also be used.

For this dish, Bartolomé-Jaime Trias Luis recommends *bomba* rice. Cultivated in the Valencia region of Spain, this type of rice is used principally for making paella. Rice is also grown on the Balearic Islands, in the marshy Albuféra region. Thin strips of cuttlefish and vegetables can be added to the rice or even some shrimp.

To serve the rice, Bartolomé-Jaime Trias Luis reserves a few whole cuttlefish bodies. These are rubbed with a spoon dipped in cuttlefish ink and then browned in a pan without fat. These hollow, fleshy, attractive "containers" are then filled with the rice and served.

Remove the heads and tentacles of the cuttlefish and wash and rinse the pocket-like bodies. Brown 12 of these whole in a dry pan and set them aside for later use. Slice the others into thin strips.

For the fish bouillon, pour the olive oil, chopped onion, fish heads and tails, leek, tomatoes and paprika into a large saucepan, with the herbs tied together in a bundle. Cover with cold water. Bring to the boil and simmer for 20 minutes. Strain.

For the cuttlefish ink rice, while the bouillon is simmering, sauté the strips of cuttlefish and diced pepper in a paella pan with a little olive oil. Add the chopped onions and tomatoes with the paprika and the green beans (reserving a few beans to garnish).

When the ingredients have become soft, add the peas and the rice. Mix together over a high heat for 3–4 minutes.

Spoon the cuttlefish ink into the rice mixture. Stir the pan vigorously over a high heat.

Add the bouillon to the rice mixture with salt and picada*. Cook for 17 minutes, then place in the oven to dry. Place three browned cuttlefish on each for the four plates and fill them with the rice mixture. Garnish with green beans and a dressing of cuttlefish ink and olive oil.*

Calamars du

Preparation time: *40 minutes*
Cooking time: *1 hour 35 minutes*
Difficulty: ★

Serves 4

3¾ lb/1.8 kg	squid
2	scallions (spring onions)
2 cloves	garlic
½ bunch	parsley
12	basil leaves
⅓ cup/80 ml	olive oil
1 tbsp/20 g	tomato concentrate
1⅔ cups/400 ml	red wine
1	small cayenne pepper
	salt

For the rice:

3	scallions (spring onions)
2½ tbsp/40 ml	olive oil
1¼ cups/250 g	long grain rice
2 cups/500 ml	fish bouillon
1 sprig	*nepita* (wild mint)
	salt and pepper

For the garnish:

1 sprig	*nepita* (wild mint)

Until recently, market day in Bastia was the time to meet in one of the small restaurants, known locally as a *cantina*, and taste the delicious cooked specialty of the day. The dishes on offer would depend on the catch, but might include gray mullet in tomato and caper sauce, rice with crab, or small fried anchovies. Squid *du pescador* (fisherman's style) was one such typical dish. Still very popular in Bastia, today it is a classic of Corsican cuisine.

Calamars du pescador is easy to prepare, suitable for any occasion, and redolent of sun-drenched Mediterranean days. The squid are gently simmered in red wine until very tender. Much enjoyed in the Mediterranean area, squid are also served broiled, fried, or stuffed. They are a relative of the cuttlefish, which can also be used for this recipe. Be sure to wash them thoroughly in cold water before use.

An essential ingredient of squid *du pescador* is the fruity flavored local olive oil. Corsican olive oil is characterized by its smooth, mild taste and excellent keeping qualities. The oil is produced only from very ripe olives that have fallen naturally from the trees.

Squid are delicious in isolation, but here, their flavor is further enhanced by the addition of a number of different herbs. *Nepita*, a peppery wild mint that grows in the Corsican *maquis*, is much used in the local cuisine. Basil leaves, with their pronounced taste of lemon and jasmine, are also much in demand.

This hearty dish is served with a timbale of rice pilaf. The rice is browned in olive oil with scallions to give a deliciously rich and tasty accompaniment.

Carefully peel the squid under running water, detaching the tentacles from the pocket-like body. Remove the "bone" (the long piece of cartilage inside the body) and the head with its eyes and beak. Rinse thoroughly. Slice the squid bodies into rings.

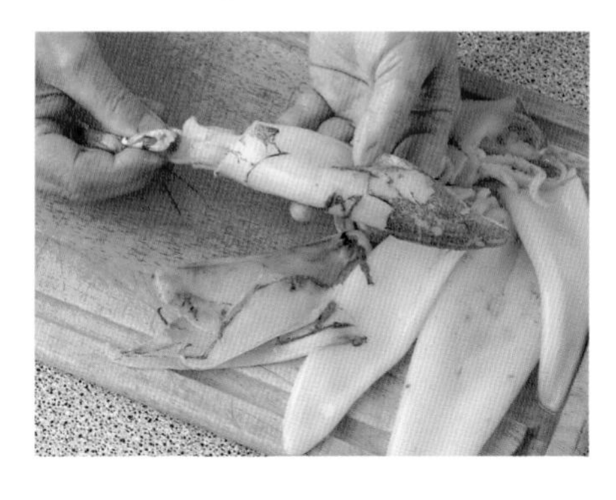

Clean and slice the scallions. Peel the garlic cloves and crush them. Strip the leaves from the sprigs of parsley and basil and chop finely. Place these ingredients in a bowl.

Heat 2½ tbsp of olive oil in a pan. Add the pieces of squid and sauté them. Remove and drain in a sieve.

Pescador

Heat the rest of the oil. Add the parsley, basil, scallions, and garlic to the pan with the drained squid. Mix together. Add the tomato concentrate and mix again. Cook for 1 minute.

Pour over the red wine. Season with salt. Add the cayenne pepper and cover the mixture with water. Cook for about 1 hour 30 minutes.

For the rice, brown the chopped scallions in the olive oil. Add the rice and brown it in the oil. Season with salt and pepper. Add the fish bouillon and bring to the boil. Simmer for 18 minutes. Sprinkle with nepita. *Arrange the squid and the rice on plates and garnish with more* nepita.

Stuffed Squid with

Preparation time: *1 hour*
Cooking time: *1 hour 30 minutes*
Difficulty: ★★★

Serves 4

For the stuffing and vegetable sauce:

16	giant shrimp
7 tbsp/100 ml	olive oil
2	leeks
2	large onions
2 heads	spinach
1 head	Swiss chard
1	cauliflower
2 or 3	eggs
2	tomatoes
4 cups/1 liter	fish bouillon

1¾ lb/800 g	whole squid
⅞ cup/100 g	flour
	oil for frying

For the basil sauce:

2 bunches	basil
¼ cup/50 g	pine nuts
2 cups/500 ml	olive oil
	salt

For the shrimp sauce:

	shrimp shells and trimmings
3½ tbsp/50 ml	brandy
3½ tbsp/50 ml	olive oil

Bartolomé-Jaime Trias Luis has never forgotten his grandmother's vegetable-stuffed squid. Dishes of this type are very popular on Mallorca, although the stuffing is more usually made with a mixture of pork, herbs, and eggs. For a special occasion, Bartolomé-Jaime Trias Luis has suggested a recipe using giant shrimps with two sauces: one of basil (known as pesto, which can also be bought ready-made), and another of seafood.

Closely related to the cuttlefish, squid range from about 8 to 16 inches/20 to 40 cm in length. They are sharp-eyed hunters which capture their prey using two long tentacles armed with suckers that emit a paralyzing poison. To escape its own predators, the squid is able to change color, and to move through the water at a speed of some 7 miles/11 km an hour. These remarkable creatures gave rise in the past to many myths about sea monsters. More recently, scientists have discovered a type of giant squid, known as *architeuthis*, living at depths of 10,000–13,000 feet/3,000–4,000 meters and reaching up to 20 feet/6 meters in length, with tentacles extending to 39 feet/12 meters.

Squid are caught on summer nights, when they are attracted to the surface by dragnets to which lights are attached. They make delicious eating once they have been thoroughly cleaned, and with the innards and skin removed.

This recipe uses a great range of vegetables. Some, mixed with the squid tentacles and the eggs, are used to stuff the squid pockets. The rest, with the addition of tomatoes and fish bouillon, are used for the sauce.

To prepare the giant shrimp used in this recipe, shell them by first removing the head and then the top two sections of the shell. Now press gently on the sides; the whole body will come out without breaking. Keep the shells and trimmings to flavor the delicious shrimp sauce.

Shell the shrimp and reserve the shells and trimmings. Remove the innards from the squid. Chop the tentacles and brown for 15 minutes in oil with the chopped leeks, onions, spinach, Swiss chard, and cauliflower. Halve this mixture and add the eggs to one half to make a stuffing.

Meanwhile, continue to cook the other half of the vegetables. Add the chopped tomatoes and the fish bouillon and cook for 30 minutes. Fill each of the squid pockets with some stuffing and one shelled shrimp. Close the end of the squid body with a cocktail stick.

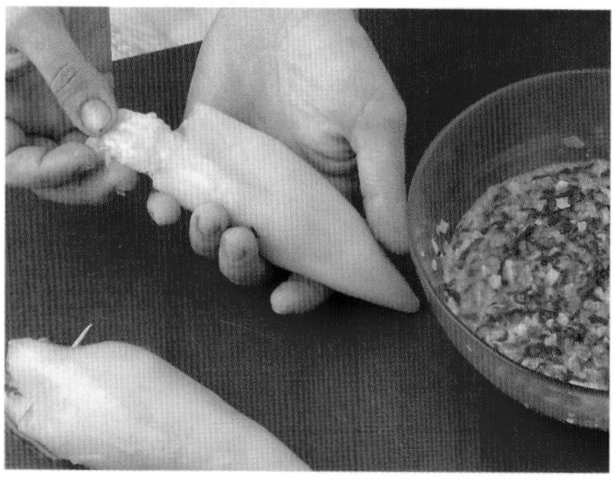

Flour the squid and fry them in a pan of very hot oil for 5 minutes, turning to ensure even browning. Remove them from the oil and place them in the pan containing the vegetable sauce. Cook them gently in the sauce for 35 minutes.

Vegetables and Shrimp

For the basil sauce, briefly poach the basil leaves, strain and reserve. Toast the pine nuts in the oven, then blend with the basil leaves, a little water, and salt. Press the mixture through a sieve, with a little more water if necessary. Finally add a little olive oil and mix thoroughly.

Place the cooked squid on a chopping board. Cut them into evenly-sized pieces about 1 inch/2–3 cm thick.

Sauté the shrimp trimmings and shells for 5 minutes in an oiled pan. Deglaze with brandy and flambé it. Now add a little water and cook for a few minutes. Strain the sauce. Arrange the pieces of stuffed squid on plates with the shrimp and basil sauces and the strained vegetables.

Sea Bream with

Preparation time: *20 minutes*
Cooking time: *10 minutes*
Difficulty: ★

Serves 4

4	sea bream, each weighing 10–11 oz/300 g
1¾ cups/200 g	flour
1 lb/400 g	broccoli
4 tbsp/60 ml	olive oil
1 cup/250 ml	*Pardu dry* (Sardinian white wine)
4 oz/100 g	green olives
	salt and pepper

For the garnish (optional):
cherry tomatoes

Sardinia has traditionally been thought of as a predominantly agricultural island, but there are many fishing villages too. The clear, clean waters surrounding its shores are rich in fish. The fish market in Oristano sells sardines, gray mullet, sea bass, scorpion fish, and sea bream. Oristano is the home of this dish of sea bream cooked in Pardu dry, a Sardinian white wine.

This typical coastal specialty marries fish with green olives and white wine. Sardinians making this dish at home generally use the local *vernaccia*, a dry, spicy white wine. For this recipe, Amerigo Murgia has chosen instead the equally admired Pardu dry.

Sea bream—a particularly fine coastal fish with delicate, white flesh—is often prepared in this way for a special occasion, when guests are invited. It should not be overcooked. Some 12–20 inches/30–50 cm in length, the sea bream is distinguished by its pink fins and a spot near the gills. In this recipe, the fish is served whole. If sea bream is not available, sea bass or gray mullet (both popular on Sardinia) can be used instead.

This easily prepared fish dish is served with broccoli. Much used in both Italian and Sardinian cooking, broccoli originated in Puglia, on the Italian mainland. Its bright green color enlivens Italian market places from fall to spring. It is rich in vitamins and minerals. Choose heads of broccoli that are firm and compact, preferably bluish-green in color. Before cooking, remove the thick stalk. After cooking, plunge the broccoli in iced water to preserve both the vitamins and its beautiful color.

First prepare the fish: remove the scales by scraping them backward with the side of knife and clean and gut them carefully (ask your fishmonger to do this, if you prefer). Wash under running water and dry with a clean cloth. Dip the fish in flour.

Separate the broccoli into medium-sized florets and remove the thick stems. Wash and cook for 3–4 minutes in a saucepan of boiling salted water.

Heat the olive oil in a very large, flat-bottomed cooking pan. Fry the fish for 3 minutes on each side.

Pardu Dry

Pour the white wine over the fish and add salt and pepper. Cook for a few minutes.

Arrange the green olives around the fish and cook very gently for a further 3 minutes.

Refresh the broccoli in a bowl of iced water. Arrange the sea bream and wine sauce on a dish. Garnish with oven-cooked cherry tomatoes.

Swordfish

Preparation time: *40 minutes*
Cooking time: *25 minutes*
Difficulty: ★

Serves 4

4 slices	swordfish
⅞ cup/100 g	flour
⅓ cup/80 ml	olive oil
1 knob	butter (optional)
5	tomatoes
1	celery heart
1 bunch	basil
1 bunch	parsley
1	onion
2 cloves	garlic
½ cup/50 g	pitted green olives
⅓ cup/40 g	capers
2 tbsp/30 g	raisins (if possible, from *Sultanina* or *Italia* grapes)
	salt and pepper

For the garnish:

celery leaves

Sicilian cuisine has been enriched throughout the island's history by encounters with other cultures. The Arabs, who settled on Sicily between the 9th and 11th centuries, introduced many delicacies that added a touch of sweetness to the local dishes. Dried fruit, sugar, and spices soon became an integral part of Sicilian cooking. Dishes evolved with a combination of sweet and sour or savory flavors, many of which are still enjoyed today.

This recipe for swordfish prepared *alla ghiotta* (*ghiotto* means "greedy") originates from Messina and Palermo. It is a traditional but delicate dish, easily prepared and suitable for any occasion.

Sicilians have always looked more to the sea than to the land for their livelihood, so it is not surprising that they have a particular fondness for fish and seafood. The very popular swordfish is still caught by traditional methods in the Ionian Sea and the Straits of Messina. Armed with a fearsome "sword," this fish can reach up to 12 feet/4 meters in length, and weigh as much as 440 lbs/200 kilos. A song by the Italian singer Domenico Modugno immortalizes the dangers involved in catching them. Known for the tenderness of its flesh, swordfish is generally sold sliced into steaks. Similar to tuna, which can also be used for this recipe, swordfish is equally delicious broiled, braised, steamed, or marinated.

This recipe features two typically Sicilian flavors: the slightly acidic capers and the sugary raisins, with their hint of Oriental cooking. Raisins are a nourishing foodstuff, generally made from seedless grape varieties. Angelo La Spina suggests using locally produced, large, ovoid *Italia* or *Sultanina* raisins.

Dip the pieces of swordfish in flour. In a pan, heat 3½ tbsp/50 ml of the oil with the knob of butter. Lightly brown the fish steaks in the pan for 3–4 minutes on each side. Remove them to a plate and soak up any excess oil with a piece of paper towel.

Peel the tomatoes and discard the seeds. Reduce them to a pulp. Wash the celery, basil, and parsley. Chop small, together with the onion and garlic cloves. Chop up the green olives.

In the pan used to cook the fish, heat the remaining olive oil and brown the onion and garlic. Add the celery, capers, and raisins. Season with salt and pepper. Cook for 5 minutes, then add the tomato pulp.

Alla Ghiotta

Add the chopped green olives to the vegetable mixture and mix carefully with a wooden spatula.

Sprinkle on the chopped parsley and basil. Mix, then cook for about 5 minutes.

Arrange the slices of swordfish in an ovenproof dish. Cover the fish with the vegetables and cook in the oven at 350 °F/180 °C for about 10 minutes. Serve the fish garnished with a few celery leaves.

Signora Ignazia's

Preparation time: *25 minutes*
Cooking time: *30 minutes*
Marinating time for tomatoes: *24 hours*
Difficulty: ★

Serves 4

1 lb/500 g	sardines
11 oz/300 g	potatoes
1	lettuce
2 tbsp/30 ml	olive oil
	salt and pepper

For the marinated tomatoes:

12	cherry tomatoes
4 level tbsp/120 g	honey
1 sprig	fresh thyme

Historically, the Sicilian nobility was known for the richness of its butter-based cuisine, while the common people used olive oil and just a few, simple ingredients. This sardine terrine, from an old family recipe, comes from the fishing communities of the island's south-eastern coast. It is a good example of Sicily's more humble, "minimalist" cuisine. In the past, the villagers would cook a dish of this kind in the communal stone oven. Despite its simplicity, this fish dish is rich in flavor. Giuseppe Barone has named it after his mother, Signora Ignazia, to whom he owes his love of cooking.

Sardines, much eaten on Sicily, appear in one of the island's most famous recipes: *pasta con le sarde*. These delicious little fish have been harvested since Antiquity and brought in to the port of Sciacca. They are readily available in the Mediterranean in the spring and summer but can, if necessary, be replaced here with fresh anchovies.

To make this terrine, sardines, slices of potato, and lettuce leaves are combined in alternating layers, with the addition of olive oil for a touch of Mediterranean sunshine. Sicilian olive oil is full-flavored and fruity, characterized by its aftertaste of sweet almonds. Cultivated mainly on the slopes of Mount Etna, olive groves are an integral part of the Sicilian landscape.

To complete the dish, baby tomatoes marinated in a mixture of honey and thyme add a touch of refinement. Sicilians enjoy sweet tastes, and these tomatoes will add an attractive splash of color to Signora Ignazia's flavorsome dish.

The day before, place the tomatoes in boiling water for 2 minutes. Drain and peel them and then put them in a bowl. Add the honey and chopped thyme and leave the mixture to marinate for 24 hours.

Prepare the sardines by cutting off the heads and tails and removing the innards. Make fillets by removing the bone (alternatively, buy fresh sardine fillets from a good fishmonger). Rinse the fillets under running water.

Peel the potatoes and slice them into very thin rounds, preferably with a mandoline.

Sardine Terrine

Wash and chop the lettuce leaves.

Grease an ovenproof dish with olive oil. Arrange a layer of lettuce leaves in the bottom of the dish. Cover this with a layer of potato slices. Season with salt and pepper.

Add a layer of sardine fillets to the dish. Season and then cover with another layer of potato and, finally, lettuce.
Cover and cook in a medium oven (350 °F/180 °C) for about 30 minutes. Turn out of the dish. Garnish the terrine with the marinated tomatoes.

Cauchi's

Preparation time:	*40 minutes*
Cooking time:	*50 minutes*
Difficulty:	★★

Serves 4

8	mackerel
$^{7}/_{8}$ cup/100 g	flour
1 cup/250 ml	olive oil
12	tomatoes
2 cloves	garlic
1$^{2}/_{3}$ cups/400 ml	white wine
1 sprig	fresh mint
2 tbsp/30 g	capers
	salt and pepper

Michael Cauchi and his wife have been running their famous restaurant in Marsascala, *Il Re del Pesce*, for eight years. Here, they have developed many delicious recipes, including this one of fish fried and simmered in a tomato and caper sauce.

Fishing on Malta is still carried out in the traditional way, using the brightly painted boats known as *luzzu*, so frequently seen on posters and postcards, and in travel books and advertisements. An eye painted on either side of the prow of each boat is believed to bring luck and ward off the evil eye.

The cream of the day's catch can be admired and bought in the fish market at Marsaxlokk. Michael Cauchi originally created this recipe using the Mediterranean fish known as bogue, or *vopa* in Maltese. This is a long, golden-colored fish with large eyes, sharp spines along the dorsal fin, and tiny pectoral fins. Here, Michael suggests using mackerel (which is much more readily available) instead. On Malta, a particularly favored variety is "Spanish mackerel" or *kavall*, which has white flesh. Unlike common mackerel, it has a striped dorsal fin, gray-blue spots over the sides and underside, and a translucid area between the eyes. Michael Cauchi suggests squeezing a lemon over the fish after frying to bring out the flavor of the flour coating.

To prepare the tomato sauce, first cut the tomatoes into quarters. Remove the skin with a knife, and chop the flesh into a pulp. This sauce will have the additional flavor of capers, which are traditionally harvested from bushes growing in the Maltese countryside.

The fish can either be covered with the tomato sauce or served on a bed of sauce to offset their appetizing browned skin.

Split the mackerel open along the underside and remove the innards. Be sure to slice open and clean away the dark red substance running along the fish's backbone too. Rinse thoroughly, and dry the fish with paper towels. Salt the insides of the fish.

Place the flour, seasoned with salt and pepper, on a plate. Carefully coat the fish with flour on both sides.

In a frying pan, fry the floured mackerel for 5 minutes in $^{4}/_{5}$ cup/200 ml of hot olive oil, turning them to brown on both sides.

Kavalli

Peel the tomatoes, remove the seeds, and chop small. Peel and crush the garlic and brown it in a pan in the remaining oil. Add the tomato to the pan with the white wine and stir vigorously over a high heat.

When the sauce is well blended, add the chopped mint leaves and capers.

Arrange the mackerel on an ovenproof dish and pour the tomato sauce over them. Cook in the oven at 320 °F/160 °C for 25 minutes.

Lobster with

Preparation time:	*30 minutes*
Cooking time:	*40 minutes*
Difficulty:	★

Serves 4

2	live lobsters
2/3 cup/150 ml	olive oil
1 lb/500 g	cherry tomatoes
3 cloves	garlic
10 sprigs	flat-leaf parsley
4 or 5 sprigs	fresh coriander
2 1/2 cups/600 ml	white wine
8 tbsp/120 g	sea urchin flesh

The Maltese chef Michael Cauchi is an expert when it comes to fish and seafood. Here, he suggests serving lobster with a delicious sauce that is commonly made not only in Malta, but also throughout the Mediterranean. To this mixture of cherry tomatoes, garlic, herbs, and olive oil, Michael Cauchi adds something special: sea urchin flesh.

Small lobsters are common around the coasts of Malta. For this recipe, Michael Cauchi uses Mediterranean lobsters (so-called "Cuban" or "Greek" varieties); however, the larger cold-water Atlantic lobsters, both American or European, will do equally well.

After cooking the tomatoes, garlic, and herbs in the olive oil, the mixture is deglazed with Maltese white wine. Grapes were introduced to Malta by the Phoenicians when they colonized the island in Antiquity. Today, the wine industry is dominated by three large vineyards. There are also a number of smaller, cooperative producers.

Sea urchins give a strong, iodine flavor to the tomato sauce. Divers are very wary of these curious spine-covered creatures. Anyone unfortunate enough to step on one will understand why. Known as *rizzi* in Maltese, they are very common in the rocky shallows near the coast. The male urchins are not eaten, but the females are eagerly sought after. Fishermen cut them in two and scoop out the orange substance inside, eating it raw, or with a squeeze of lemon.

Be sure to select very fresh sea urchins. Once opened, it is easy to remove the flesh with a spoon. There is really no substitute for the unique contrast between the flavors of the sea urchin and the lobster, so if you dislike sea urchin, simply serve the tomato sauce on its own.

Bend back the tails of the lobsters and place them on their backs. Split them lengthwise down the middle. Separate the two halves. Clean the insides under running water.

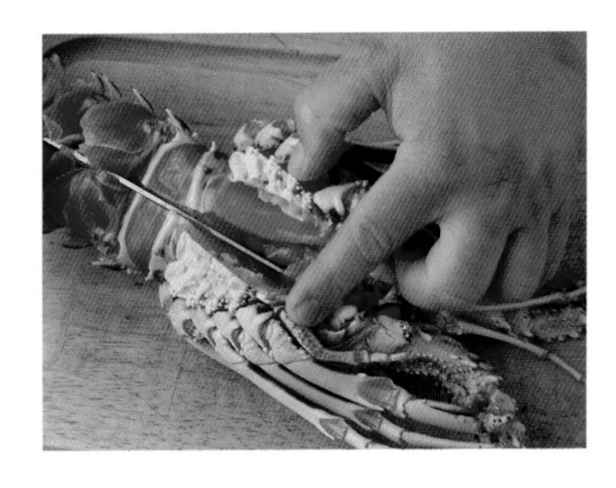

Fry the lobster halves for 5 minutes in two thirds of the oil, covering the pan with a lid. Then turn them over and brown the other side. Transfer them to an ovenproof dish and cook in a moderate oven for another 20 minutes.

Brown the cherry tomatoes for 5 minutes in the remaining oil, together with the chopped garlic, parsley, and coriander. Deglaze with the white wine. Simmer for 5 minutes and then blend in a food processor (reserving a few cooked tomatoes and parsley leaves to garnish).

Sea Urchins

Strain the sauce through a sieve into a saucepan.

Add the sea urchin flesh to the tomato sauce and stir.

Cover the lobster halves with the sauce. Garnish with cherry tomatoes and parsley leaves and eat hot.

Grouper with

Preparation time: *35 minutes*
Cooking time: *50 minutes*
Salting time for the okra: *1–2 hours*
Difficulty: ★

Serves 4

1¼ lb/600 g	fresh okra
	juice of 1 lemon
2 lb/1 kg	grouper
4 oz/100 g	onion
1 clove	garlic
7 oz/200 g	tomatoes
⅓ cup/80 ml	extra-virgin olive oil
	salt and pepper

To garnish:

2 tbsp/30 g	flat-leaf parsley

The Cretans living in the coastal areas of the island are skilled in adapting the harvest of the sea to their daily menu. One of the favorite dishes in Malia, Sitia, and Rethymnon is fish with okra, known locally as *psari me bamiès*.

For this version of the recipe, Michalis Markakis has used fillets of grouper fish, but sea bream or red snapper would be equally suitable. The grouper is a large fish with delicate flesh. Its sides are brown with brownish-yellow patches, and it has a protuberant mouth. On Crete, they are sold when still quite small (2–4 lb/1–2 kg) and can be cooked whole. The fish can be served whole and eaten without difficulty, as the central bone lifts out easily.

Much enjoyed all over Greece, okra or *bamya* are long, green vegetables, about the size of a small gherkin. Other names for this vegetable are "Greek horn" and "ladies' finger." Okra is also a distinctive feature of African and Caribbean cooking. Its flavor combines especially well with tomatoes and onions.

The flesh of the okra produces a gelatinous substance, which is useful for thickening sauces. To eliminate this when it is not needed, Cretan cooks sprinkle the okra with salt and lemon juice, vinegar, or green grape juice, depending on the time of year. This draws out the gelatin, shrinking the vegetables and making them less likely to fall apart when cooked. The acidity of the lemon juice or vinegar also makes them slightly quicker to cook in the oven. They should be rinsed before using.

This dish is usually sprinkled with parsley before being placed in the oven. Michalis Markakis recommends adding the parsley after cooking, however, thus preserving its bright green color, flavor, and vitamins.

Rinse the okra. Clean them by scraping off the tiny pointed leaves at the tip and the prickly hairs.

Place the okra on a dish and pour over the juice of half a lemon. Salt generously. Leave them to give up their gelatin for 1–2 hours, then rinse them in running water.

Cut the fish fillets into individual portions. Peel and chop the onion and garlic. Peel and blend the tomatoes to make a pulp.

Okra

In a frying pan, brown the chopped garlic and onion for 5 minutes in the olive oil. Deglaze with lemon juice. Add the puréed tomato to the pan and season with salt and pepper. Simmer the sauce for 15 minutes.

Place the okra and pieces of fish in a shallow ovenproof dish. Pour over the tomato sauce. Cook in a moderate oven (340 °F/170 °C) for 30 minutes.

When the fish and vegetables are cooked, sprinkle the dish with chopped parsley and serve piping hot.

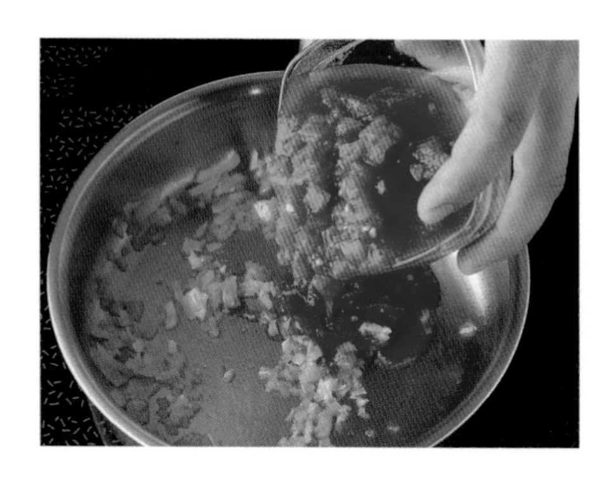

Cod and Leeks

Preparation time: *25 minutes*
Cooking time: *40 minutes*
Desalting time for cod: *overnight*
Difficulty: ★

Serves 4

2 lb/1 kg	salt cod
7 oz/200 g	potatoes
2	onions
1 lb/500 g	leeks
2 sticks	celery
4	medium tomatoes
1¼ cups/300 ml	virgin olive oil
1¾ cups/200 g	flour
	salt and pepper

For the garnish:

3 bunches	flat-leaf parsley

Yachni is a dish of stewed vegetables with fresh tomatoes. In this popular Cretan recipe, it is combined with salt cod and leeks to give a well-flavored dish typical of the island's cuisine. Similar assortments of strongly flavored vegetables are eaten at most Cretan meals.

Today, salt cod is found on the menu in all parts of Greece. Available all year round, it is also cheap. While the Cretans who live on the coast have always enjoyed a plentiful supply of fish and seafood, the inhabitants of the mountain areas of the island traditionally used dried, salted cod imported from Iceland and Scandinavia, prepared with fresh vegetables, beans, and wild herbs. Preserved in this hard, dry state, salt cod should be cut into large pieces and soaked in regular changes of cold water for 24–48 hours before cooking. Avoid having to change the water too often by placing the fish pieces in a sieve or wire basket and immersing this in a large bowl of water so that it does not touch the bottom of the container. In this way, the salt will fall to the bottom of the bowl without resalting the fish. When the fish is ready, rinse it well under running water before cooking.

The quantity of leeks used in this dish is twice that of the other vegetables. The color and taste of the tomatoes also play an important role. Celery is included for its aromatic qualities. In place of leeks, the recipe could also be made with cauliflower florets. The vegetables can also be cooked together with the cod, without any precooking. The resulting dish will be lighter but less attractive.

Prepare the cod the day before by cutting off the fins and splitting the fish lengthwise down the middle. Cut it into pieces about 4 inches/10 cm across. Place these to soak for 12 hours in a bowl of cold water.

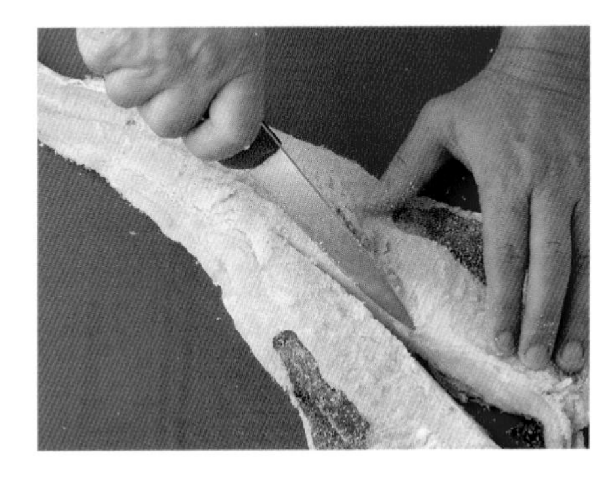

Peel, wash, and dice the potatoes. Chop the onions. Clean and slice the leeks and celery. Wash the tomatoes and cut into small dice.

Brown the onions, leeks, celery, potatoes, and tomatoes in a saucepan in a little olive oil for 10–15 minutes, stirring constantly.

with Yachni

Rinse and dry the pieces of cod with some paper towel. Pour the flour onto a plate and thoroughly coat the cod pieces.

Heat some oil in a pan. When it is very hot, add the cod pieces and fry them, turning to brown both sides.

Add the cod to the saucepan of cooked vegetables. Season with salt and pepper. Cook for a further 15 minutes. Serve very hot in shallow bowls, garnished with the parsley.

Rice with Rock Fish

Preparation time: *45 minutes*
Cooking time: *1 hour 10 minutes*
Difficulty: ★★★

Serves 4

For the fish bouillon:

	shrimp shells
4/5 cup/200 ml	olive oil
2 or 3 sprigs	chervil
1	bay leaf
2 or 3 sprigs	parsley
1	leek
1	scallion (spring onion)
1/2	onion
	fish bones
2 tbsp/30 g	paprika
3 or 4	Mallorcan tomatoes

For the rice:

8	mussels
8	clams
8	small cooked shrimp
1	squid
1	scorpion fish
1	red gurnard
2	weever fish
1	sea bream
7 tbsp/100 ml	olive oil
1 cup/200 g	rice
2 oz/50 g	sugar peas

For the *picada*:

1/2 bunch	parsley
2 cloves	garlic
2	dried *ñora* peppers

The inhabitants of the fishing villages of the Balearic Islands frequently made use of a combination of fish in soups or rice dishes. Rice with rock fish and seafood, known locally as *arroz de pescado de costa y marisco*, is a particular favorite. The ingredients will depend on the day's catch. Oscar Martínez Plaza generally uses scorpion fish and a number of local rock fish (*sardos*, *rata*, and others). In place of these, we suggest using red gurnard, sea bream, and weever fish.

The red gurnard can easily be recognized by its large, domed head, the bulging eyes near the top of the skull, and its orange-red cone-shaped body. It lives in the sand or mud at depths of around 490 feet/150 meters. By moving its swim bladder, it is able to make a kind of growling sound, hence its name (*grondin* in French, from the verb *gronder* meaning "to rumble"). The red scorpion fish has a large head, and is covered with spines. Very common in the Mediterranean, it lives at a depth of 65–165 feet/20–50 meters, hiding in the sand or seaweed-covered rocks.

Toward the end of the cooking time, a mixture of ground herbs and spices known as *picada* is mixed into the rice and fish. Garlic and parsley are combined with *ñora*, a mild-flavored, dark-red, rounded pepper. The people of the Balearics hang these peppers outside their houses to dry in the sun. Before use, soak them and scrape the flesh with a knife. If you are lucky enough to find any, enrich the *picada* with the liver of a monkfish.

To serve this dish, reserve a few pieces of fish, shrimp, and squid, and brown these separately. Place the rice in shallow bowls, arranging some squid in the center surrounded by the browned fish and shrimp, and some sugar peas.

Soak the ñora *peppers in some water. Scald the mussels and clams, then plunge them into cold water, and remove the shells. Peel the shrimp. Clean and rinse the squid, then cut it into rings. Fillet the fish. Set these ingredients aside.*

For the fish bouillon, brown the heads and shells of the shrimp in a little hot oil with a bouquet garni of chervil, bay leaf, and parsley. Add the roughly-chopped leek, scallion, and onion, together with the fish bones.

Add the paprika and the quartered tomatoes. Cook for a few minutes, then add 12 cups/3 liters of cold water. Simmer for 20 minutes. Strain the bouillon.

and Seafood

For the picada*, use a pestle and mortar to grind together the chopped parsley, the garlic, and the flesh of the soaked ñora pepper.*

Heat a little oil in a saucepan, and quickly brown the fish fillets and the squid. Add 10 cups of the strained bouillon, and bring to the boil.

Add the raw rice to the bouillon. Cook for 5 minutes, then add the picada *and sugar peas. Cook for a further 20 minutes, then serve hot with the fish, as described above.*

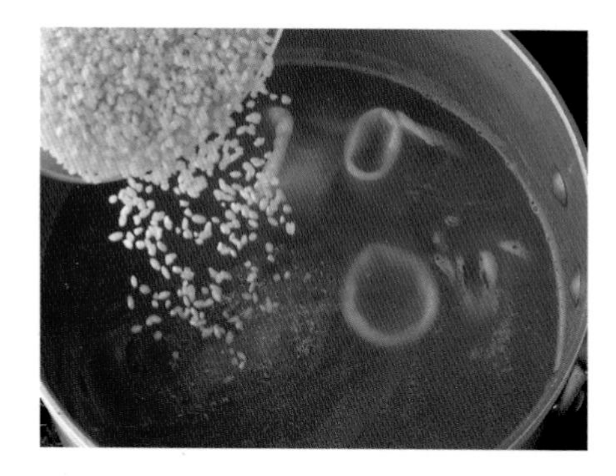

Stuffed Sardines

Preparation time: *30 minutes*
Cooking time: *45 minutes*
Difficulty: ★

Serves 4

12	sardines, 5 oz/150 g each
1 bunch	mint
1	*brocciu* (Corsican cheese, approximately 14 oz/400 g
2	eggs
5 oz/150 g	Corsican *tomme* (cheese)
	salt and pepper

For the tomato sauce:

1	onion
3½ tbsp/50 ml	olive oil
½ bunch	parsley
1 clove	garlic
1 lb/500 g	tomatoes
3½ tbsp/50 ml	white wine
	salt and pepper

For the garnish:

mint leaves

Typical of the Corsican coast, this dish of sardines filled with *brocciu* cheese would have been a regular favorite at any fisherman's family table. A wonderful combination of ingredients from the sea and the mountains, this specialty is easy to prepare, and is often served accompanied by spinach or Swiss chard.

Traditional fishing methods are still used on Corsica. Renowned for their delicious flavor, the sardines that abound in the waters of the Mediterranean in the spring and summer are caught in trawl nets. Fairly large fish should be used for this dish, as these are the most suitable for stuffing. Whole squid "pockets" are a delicious alternative.

Many Corsican dishes involve the use of *brocciu* in a stuffing. Traditionally made by shepherds from the whey of goat's or ewe's milk, mixed with whole milk, water, and salt, this cheese is creamy, light, and mild, and much used in cooking. It has been awarded a coveted French *appellation d'origine contrôlée*, guaranteeing its quality and authenticity.

The taste of the sardines in this summery dish is enhanced by the refreshing flavor of wild mint, commonly found throughout the Mediterranean. Believed in Antiquity to have calming properties, we know today that it is rich in calcium, iron, and vitamins. Choose mint with firm stems and a good green color. If you have more than you need, you can dry it by placing it in a well-ventilated place away from the light. It can then be chopped finely and stored in a glass jar.

The finishing touch to this colorful and delicious dish is the tomato sauce, usually made from home-grown vegetables.

Prepare the sardines. Break off the head, then remove the innards and central bone. Rinse in running water (whole fresh, filleted sardines can also be bought at good fishmongers).

Wash the bunch of mint. Detach the leaves and slice finely with a knife.

Put the brocciu *in a bowl and mash it together with the eggs and the chopped mint. Season with salt and pepper. Mix well.*

with Brocciu

For the sauce, brown the chopped onion in the olive oil. Add the chopped parsley and garlic. Add the pulped tomatoes and season with salt and pepper. Pour over the white wine and cook the mixture for about 15 minutes. Blend the sauce in a food processor.

Place the filleted sardines on the worktop. Using a spoon, fill them with the cheese stuffing, propping them up one against the other on a plate, to prevent the sauce from spilling out.

Pour the tomato sauce into an ovenproof dish. Arrange the sardines in the dish. Scatter with shavings of Corsican tomme *cheese. Cook at 350 °F/180 °C for about 30 minutes. Serve the sardines on plates with the sauce. Garnish with the mint leaves.*

Cuttlefish in

Preparation time:	*20 minutes*
Cooking time:	*35 minutes*
Difficulty:	★

Serves 4

2 lb/1 kg	small, cleaned and gutted cuttlefish
4/5 cup/200 ml	virgin olive oil
7 tbsp/100 ml	red wine vinegar
2 level tbsp/50 g	honey
3 1/2 tbsp/50 g	fresh rosemary
	salt and pepper

A traditional dish served on Crete, cuttlefish in *oxymeli* sauce is served during *megali sarakosti*, the period of seven weeks' fasting leading up to Easter. While meat and its derivatives (butter, milk, eggs, and cheese) may not be eaten on fast days, fish is permitted.

To speed up the preparation of this dish, it can be made with ready-prepared cuttlefish bodies, either fresh or frozen. If these are not available, remove the head and innards of the fresh cuttlefish, followed by the skin and the hard inner "bone." Rinse the mantles in running water, turning them inside out like the finger of a glove, but taking care not to tear them.

After rinsing the cuttlefish, dry them well with paper towels to prevent them from spitting when put in the hot oil. Even so, stand well back from the pan, or cover it, when frying.

Cuttlefish is ideal for this recipe since the flesh remains firm even when cooked. Squid can also be used but should be floured beforehand so that they will brown without collapsing in the pan.

Oxymeli sauce is commonly used on Crete with seafood, fish, snails, and salads of wild herbs and leaves. The Cretan honey, *meli Kritis*, gives it a delicate, sweet-sour flavor. According to legend, Zeus spent his childhood on Crete, hidden on Mount Ida. He was fed on goat's milk and honey that the bees brought to his lips. Honey has been an essential ingredient of Cretan cooking for centuries, and is used as a sweetener and in medicines.

In this sauce, the rosemary blends perfectly with the virgin olive oil so characteristic of many Cretan dishes. The small, needle-like leaves of this herb, used in Greek cuisine since Antiquity, will enliven the *oxymeli* sauce.

Open out the cuttlefish bodies and cut them into large rectangles.

Heat the olive oil in a pan. Add the pieces of cuttlefish and brown them for 10 minutes over a high heat.

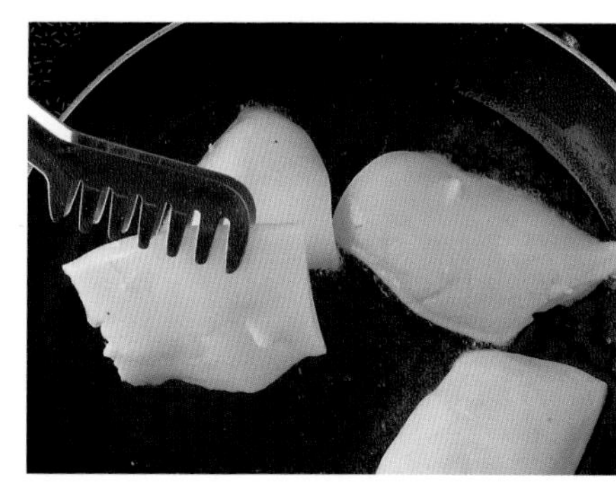

Remove the pieces of fried cuttlefish and arrange them in a shallow ovenproof dish. Retain the pan with the cooking oil.

Almond Sauce

Pour the rest of the vinegar into the mortar and mix with a wooden spatula.

Pour the flour onto a plate and flour both sides of the tuna fish.

Melt the butter with the rest of the olive oil in a frying pan. Fry the tuna in this. Drain off any excess oil. Season the fish with salt and pepper. Arrange the slices on plates, covering them with the almond sauce. Garnish with some olive oil with chopped parsley.

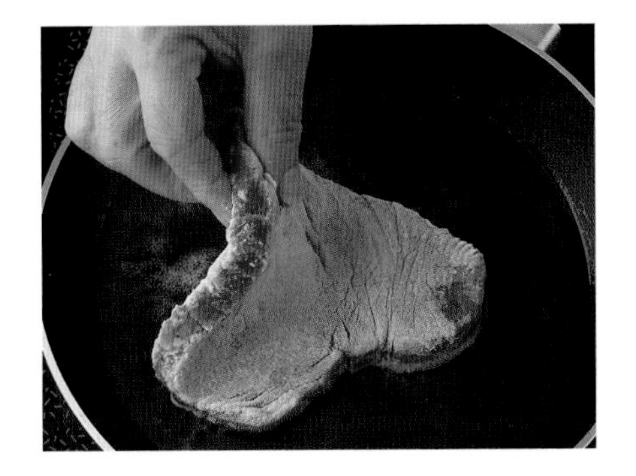

Tians of Sea Bass with

Preparation time:	*40 minutes*
Cooking time:	*40 minutes*
Difficulty:	★

Serves 4

12	spinach leaves (to wrap the tians)
1¼ lb/600 g	sea bass fillets
	salt and freshly ground pepper

For the stuffing:

7 oz/200 g	spinach leaves
11 oz/300 g	*brocciu* (Corsican soft cheese)
½ bunch	parsley
1 sprig	*persia* (wild marjoram)
1	egg
	salt and pepper

For the tomato coulis:

12	basil leaves
1	scallion (spring onion)
5 sprigs	parsley
2 cloves	garlic
3½ tbsp/50 ml	olive oil
11 oz/300 g	ripe tomatoes
	salt and pepper

For the garnish (optional):

cherry tomatoes
basil leaves
black olives

This elegant dish of sea bass with *brocciu* and a tomato coulis uses typically Corsican ingredients. Vincent Tabarani has created a truly delicious recipe that combines the best of the island's seas and mountains. Corsica's popular *brocciu* cheese stuffing is combined here with fish. Easy to prepare, this is convivial dish to share with friends.

In the old days on Corsica, a young bride would be welcomed by her mother-in-law with a gift of a bowl of *caghiatu*, milk curds. This country custom emphasizes the importance attached throughout history, to the local cheese, *brocciu*. Still made using traditional methods from a mixture of the whey and whole milk of goats or ewes, the cheese now holds a coveted *appellation d'origine contrôlée*, guaranteeing its authenticity and quality. It has a very mild taste, and can be used in cooking, for both sweet and savory dishes.

Stuffing made with *brocciu* and a hint of *persia* (wild marjoram) is a classic of Corsican cuisine. It is most commonly used as a filling for pasta envelopes, but marries equally well with fish, as will be seen here. Sea bass, much prized by the people of the Mediterranean for its delicate, firm flesh, is also found in the Atlantic. Other fish that can be used for this recipe are dentex or trout, the latter being common in Corsican streams.

The fish tians are parcels of stuffed fish wrapped in spinach leaves. Coming originally from Persia, spinach can be found on the market stalls in both spring and fall. Swiss chard leaves may also be used. With their accompanying tomato coulis, these fish tians make a most attractive and colorful dish.

Wash the spinach leaves. In salted water, blanch the spinach for the stuffing, followed by the 12 leaves to be used to wrap the tians. Refresh the latter in iced water.

Prepare the coulis by browning the basil and chopped scallion, the chopped stalks of the parsley (reserve the leaves), and the crushed garlic in the olive oil. Add the chopped tomatoes and season with salt and pepper. Cook for about 30 minutes, then blend in a food processor.

For the stuffing, mix together in a bowl the brocciu, *parsley leaves,* persia, *and chopped spinach leaves. Add salt and pepper and then the egg. Mash the mixture together with a fork.*

Brocciu and Tomato Coulis

Check the bass fillets for bones and remove these. Cut the fish into thin pieces weighing about 2 oz/50 g each.

Spread the 12 spinach leaves on a flat surface. Place one fillet of fish on each leaf. Season. Cover with stuffing. Place a second piece of fish on top.

Wrap the fish in the spinach leaf. Place the completed parcels in a dish and pour over the tomato coulis. Cook in a medium oven (350 °F/180 °C) for 8–10 minutes. Serve the tians with the tomato coulis on plates.

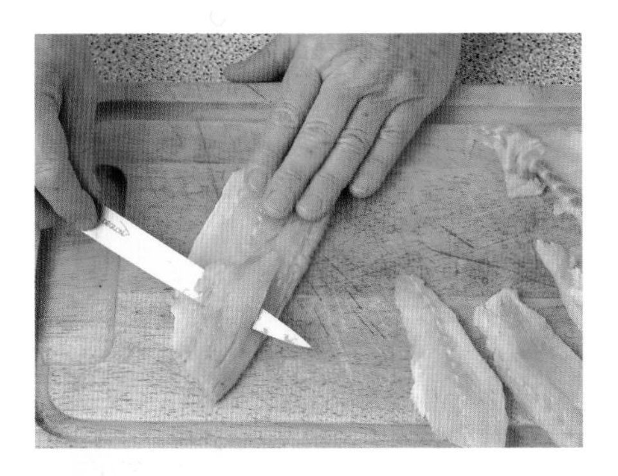

Meat & Poultry

Kid Alla Stretta

Preparation time:	*40 minutes*
Cooking time:	*1 hour 5 minutes*
Difficulty:	★

Serves 4

½	kid
3 tbsp/50 g	flour
¼ cup/60 ml	olive oil
5 cloves	garlic
½ bunch	parsley
8 tbsp/150 g	tomato concentrate
1¼ cups/300 ml	*nielluccio* (red wine)
2	bay leaves
	salt and pepper

For the *pulenda*:

1½ cups/250 g	chestnut flour
	salt

For the garnish:

	bay leaves

Cooked traditionally at Easter time, this dish is very popular on Corsica. Using goat's meat, chestnuts, and other local ingredients, it celebrates the wonderful flavors of Corsican produce.

Still close to their pastoral roots, the Corsicans have retained many customs from an earlier age. In the past, for the inhabitants of the mountainous Niolo region, sheep and goat husbandry represented the sole source of income. The meat of young goats, or kids, is a particular favorite. The kid will always be male, because the female kids are reared for milking. Kid is only available in the period leading up to the festivals of Christmas and Easter; a suckling lamb can be substituted at other times of year.

Cooked very slowly in red wine, the meat absorbs the flavors of the different ingredients. The cooking liquid is reduced, giving a rich *stretta* sauce. Serge Fazzini has chosen to use a typically Corsican wine for this sauce, *nielluccio*. This distinctive, deep red wine has been known since Antiquity. A red wine from the south-east of mainland France can be used in its place.

This hearty dish provides an opportunity to try Corsica's polenta, or *pulenda*. Made with chestnut flour, it has a slightly bittersweet taste. Sweet chestnut trees grow in the Castagniccia area, and chestnuts play an important role in traditional Corsican cooking.

As a basic foodstuff since the earliest times, chestnuts are cultivated on Corsica for flour, or to be cooked and eaten like other vegetables. Still gathered by hand, they are smoked for a month before being ground into flour. Chestnut flour is available in Corsican groceries between December and May, but cornstarch can be used in its place if necessary.

Prepare the kid meat. Divide the ribs into cutlets and cut the leg into large pieces. Flour the meat.

Heat the olive oil in a large pan. Brown the pieces of meat for 1 minute on each side. Season with salt and pepper and set aside.

Peel the garlic clove and wash the parsley. Chop both ingredients and mix them together. Put the tomato concentrate into a bowl with the garlic and parsley. Add the red wine and ⅔ cup/150 ml water. Mix together.

with Chestnut Pulenda

Put the pieces of meat in an ovenproof dish. Pour over the wine mixture and add the bay leaves. Cover the dish with aluminum foil, and cook in a medium oven (350 °F/180 °C) for about 1 hour.

For the pulenda, *sieve the chestnut flour into a bowl.*

Heat 1¼ cups/300 ml salted water. When it boils, add the chestnut flour. Cook for 3 minutes, stirring with a wooden spatula. Tip the mixture into a cloth and allow to cool a little. Arrange the pieces of meat on plates with a slice of pulenda. *Garnish with a bay leaf.*

Kid with Askolibri

Preparation time: *20 minutes*
Cooking time: *55 minutes*
Difficulty: ★

Serves 4

2 lb/1 kg	*askolibri (scolymus hispanicus)*
2	onions
⅔ cup/150 ml	virgin olive oil
2 lb/1 kg	kid cutlets

7 tbsp/100 ml	white wine
2	eggs
	juice of 1 lemon
	salt and pepper

For the garnish:

1 bunch	dill

Generally eaten in the springtime, this festive dish combines the tender meat of goat kid with the fresh stalks of a species of thistle, *scolymus hispanicus*, in a typically Greek sauce made with eggs and lemon juice.

As long ago as the Minoan period, 4,000 to 5,000 years ago, sheep, goats, and cattle were reared on the island of Crete. Today, lamb and goat are the Cretans' favorite meats. Since both are particularly good at Easter time, either is suitable for this recipe. The meat of Cretan goats has an especially fine flavor, doubtless due to their pastures in the high mountainous areas, where they graze on a number of different herbs and aromatic plants. The recipe calls for cutlets, since these look attractive when served, but other cuts of meat can be used.

Askolibri give great individuality to this dish. These wild plants have long, prickly stems that are slightly curved and furnished with very small toothed leaves. Resembling miniature artichokes, they grow as bushes in the mountains of Crete. They were already known as a foodstuff some 3,000 years ago, at the time of Homer. Several centuries later, the scholars Pliny and Dioscorides recommended boiling their roots in wine to make a body wash. Today, the leaves and roots are generally boiled and then eaten as a salad. They are even cultivated on a small scale on Crete, to sell in the local markets. For this recipe, dandelion leaves or wild chicory can be used as a substitute.

Avgolemono sauce, used in the preparation of many Greek soups and stews, should be made with care to prevent the eggs from curdling in the lemon juice. Once it has been added to the meat, place the pan on the heat, shaking it as you do so. Then serve without delay.

Cut off the bases of the askolibri *stems. Scrape off the prickles and small leaves, keeping only the curving stems. Cut them into small pieces.*

Peel and chop the onions. Brown them in the olive oil, then add the cutlets, browning them on both sides. Pour on the wine and let it bubble to evaporate for 5 minutes over a high heat.

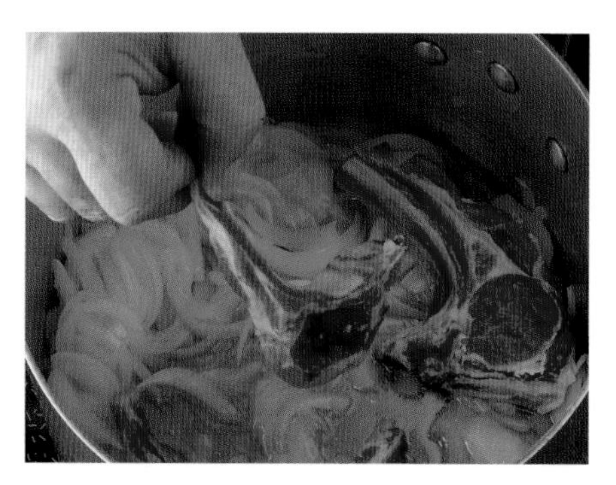

Blanch the askolibri *stems for 5 minutes in boiling water, then drain.*

in Avgolemono Sauce

Add the askolibri *to the cutlets and season with salt and pepper. Mix together and cook for 5 minutes. Pour in just enough water to cover. Put a lid on the pan and cook for 30 minutes.*

Beat 2 egg whites until firm. Beat the yolks in a separate bowl, then combine them with the whites. Add the lemon juice, then gradually add some of the liquid in which the meat was cooked, beating the sauce all the while.

Just before serving, pour the sauce into the pan containing the meat and mix vigorously. Garnish with dill and serve immediately.

Cinu Ri Jaddu

Preparation time:	*1 hour*
Cooking time:	*1 hour 5 minutes*
Difficulty:	★★★

Serves 4

1	small to medium-sized chicken (preferably a young rooster)
1 lb/400 g	mussels
2 cloves	garlic
1²/₃ cups/300 g	couscous
1 knob	butter
5 tbsp/70 g	mint leaves

1½ oz/40 g	pitted green olives
1	onion
4 oz/100 g	tomatoes
⅓ cup/40 g	ground toasted almonds
2 tbsp/30 ml	olive oil
	juice and peel of 4 lemons
3½ tbsp/50 ml	white wine
	salt and black pepper

For the garnish:

	lemon peel
	bay leaf (optional)

In Sicilian dialect, *cinu ri jaddu* means "stuffed cockerel." A rich, traditional dish from the area around Trapani, it is generally eaten at Easter and Christmas. Requiring patience and care in preparation, it offers a delicious combination of flavors from sea and land.

The most difficult part of this recipe is preparing the bird, since it needs to have its bones completely removed before stuffing. If you find this a problem, ask your butcher to do it. On Sicily, it is usual to select a rooster weighing 4½–6½ lb/2–3 kg. For this recipe, Giuseppe Barone has used a smaller bird, ideal for four people.

The substantial stuffing is made up of ingredients typical of the Sicilian countryside: mint, olives, onions, tomatoes, ground almonds, and semolina. To these are added mussels (*cozze*). These *cozze*, available in all the main markets, play an important role in the success of this dish.

Be careful to choose only firmly-closed mussels that have not dried out. Throw away any shells that are broken or partly opened. Before cooking the mussels, remove the beard, then scrub them under running water. The water in which they are cooked should be strained before being added to the stuffing.

Couscous was introduced to the Mediterranean islands several centuries ago by Tunisian fishermen, and is much used in Sicilian cooking today, in the regions around Trapani and on the island of Pantelleria. A particularly good version of couscous with fish originates from Pantelleria. Couscous grains are particularly suitable for stuffings such as the one described here, as they become deliciously impregnated with the flavors of the other ingredients. Some Sicilians prefer to use rice or various types of small pasta.

Carefully remove the bones from the body of the bird by cutting down the spine. Remove this, together with the breastbone and ribs.

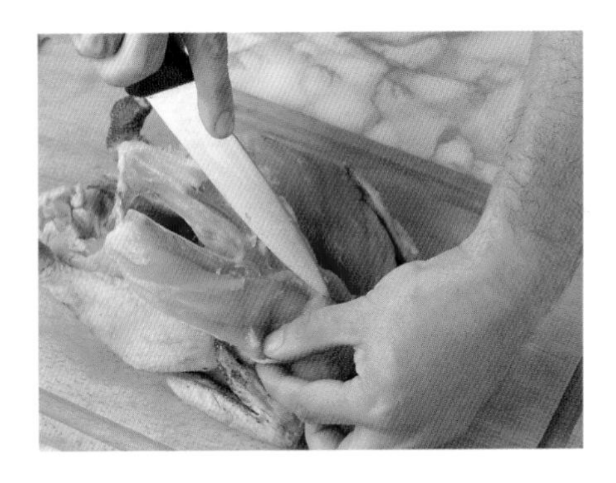

Clean the mussels. Place them in a deep cooking pan with the unpeeled, whole garlic cloves and a cup or two of water for cooking (the mussels should steam rather than boil in the water). When cooked, strain the cooking liquid and reserve. Remove the mussels from their shells.

Pour the couscous into the cooking liquid from the mussels and cook for about 4 minutes. Add the butter and mix it in.

For the stuffing, add the mint, olives, and chopped onion to the cooked couscous. Add the shelled mussels, pulped tomatoes, and ground almonds. Season with salt and pepper. Add more couscous grains if the mixture seems too liquid.

Season the bird, then fill it with stuffing. Using a needle and kitchen string, sew up the bird's body cavity. Brush it with olive oil. Place it on a rack in the oven and cook for 30 minutes, collecting the juices in an ovenproof dish placed underneath the bird.

Now place the bird in the dish containing the juices. Pour over the lemon juice and lemon peel. Return to the oven for 30 minutes at 320 °F/160 °C. Pour off and strain the juices. Deglaze with white wine. Serve the chicken with the sauce. Garnish with a bay leaf and lemon peel.

Pork Chops

Preparation time:	*35 minutes*
Cooking time:	*10 minutes*
Difficulty:	⭑

Serves 4

1	pork loin
¼ cup/60 ml	olive oil
1	onion
3 cups/150 g	fresh breadcrumbs
1 bunch	parsley
pinch	grated nutmeg
2	eggs
3 oz/80 g	grated pecorino
½ cup/50 g	flour
1 knob	butter (optional)
	salt and pepper

For the garnish:

parsley
cherry tomatoes (optional)

This pork dish is named for Chiaromonte, a small town a few miles from Ragusa, in the heart of Baroque Sicily. The local inhabitants are justly proud of this richly-flavored, time-honored country specialty. Easy to make, it can be eaten on any occasion, although pork has strong associations with Christmas festivities on Sicily. Pork chops are traditionally stuffed, and served with lentils, vegetables, or potatoes. The tender meat is cut on the bone from a loin joint, and served well cooked.

Vegetarian stuffings such as the one described here are much used on Sicily. The ingredients are very simple: onion, breadcrumbs, eggs, pecorino cheese, and parsley. Breadcrumbs, made from stale bread, are a common feature of Sicilian country cooking. They are used to make a dish more nourishing and substantial, or to bind sauces.

Countless invaders throughout history have fought over Sicily, and left their influence on Sicilian cuisine. When the Arabs arrived in the 9th century, they brought with them exotically scented spices, such as the nutmeg used here. Nutmegs are ovoid in shape, about the size of an almond. Often used in milk dishes, this spice has a powerful taste. It is always best to keep a whole nutmeg and grate it as required, since ready-ground nutmeg quickly loses its aroma.

The rather surprising use of butter with olive oil in the cooking of meat and fish is said by some people to date from the 19th century, when French chefs were often employed by the Sicilian nobility.

Prepare the pork loin by cutting it into chops (ask your butcher to do this if you prefer).

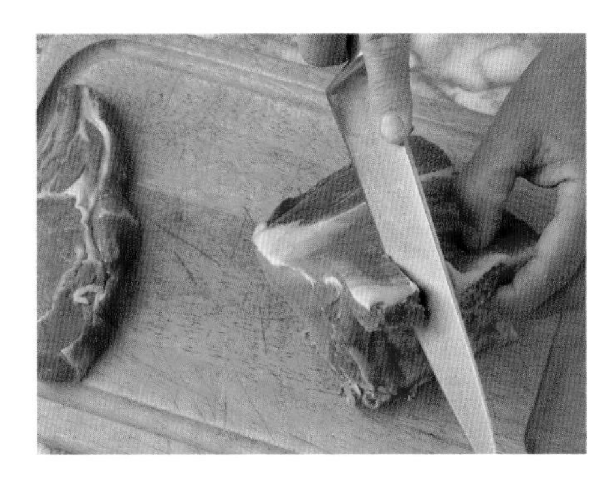

Slit open the chops horizontally for stuffing.

Gently soften the chopped onion in a pan with half of the olive oil. Add the breadcrumbs and season with salt and pepper. Mix together with the onion. Add the chopped parsley.

Alla Chiaromonte

Take the pan off the heat and add the nutmeg and eggs. Mix together thoroughly. Add the grated pecorino. Leave the stuffing to cool.

Carefully fill the pork chops with spoonfuls of stuffing.

Sew the two sides of the chops together with kitchen string. Flour the meat and cook in a pan with the other half of the olive oil and butter. Remove the string. Serve the chops garnished with cherry tomatoes and chopped parsley.

Stuffed Zucchini

Preparation time:	*40 minutes*
Cooking time:	*1 hour 5 minutes*
Difficulty:	★★

Serves 4

4 large round	zucchini (courgettes)
4 cups/1 liter	beef bouillon
1 tbsp/20 g	tomato concentrate
7 oz/200 g	carrots
1	kohlrabi
3	potatoes
1 stick	celery
7 oz/200 g	fresh peas
1	bay leaf
	salt and pepper

For the stuffing:

5 cloves	garlic
2	large onions
7 oz/200 g	bacon
3½ tbsp/50 ml	corn oil
1 lb/500 g	ground beef
1 lb/500 g	ground pork
4 cups/200 g	fresh white breadcrumbs
1½ cups/150 g	dried breadcrumbs
1 bunch	flat-leaf parsley
9 oz/250 g	grated parmesan
3	eggs

The plots of land devoted to vegetable growing on Malta are relatively small, but they are cultivated with great care. Shoppers at the local markets are presented with a magnificent display of round zucchini, cauliflowers, eggplants, and red and green bell peppers.

Stuffed zucchini in bouillon was traditionally a popular dish among the poorer country people. The meat stuffing was supplemented with cheaper ingredients such as bread, often used in Maltese cooking. Nothing was wasted in the preparation of what was a complete meal: the cooking liquid was consumed as a soup, while the stuffed zucchini provided the main course.

In Maltese, this dish is called *qarabali mimli*. *Qarabali* are round zucchini (a relative of the squash), about the size of a tennis ball or slightly larger, and green in color. These are commonly grown on Malta and generally eaten stuffed or boiled. They are stuffed not only with meat but also with tuna fish or soft cheeses, such as feta or ricotta, mixed with herbs. More recently, imported zucchini have begun to appear in Maltese markets.

The tradition of using bacon to enrich the stuffing is a legacy of the lengthy period during which Malta remained in English hands. As Johann Chetcuti observes, the island's English community has introduced a number of other delicacies that are still eaten here today: toasted sandwiches, Christmas pudding, beef curry, and fried eggs with French fries.

As an alternative to cooking the zucchini in beef bouillon, braise or roast them in a covered pan with a little white wine, water, and lemon juice. The addition of an assortment of small, brightly colored vegetables to the bouillon will improve its taste and look attractive when the zucchini are served.

Brown the chopped garlic, onions, and bacon in the oil in a large saucepan for 5 minutes. Mix in the ground beef and pork and continue cooking for about 10 minutes.

Add the fresh and dried breadcrumbs to the meat, together with the chopped parsley and the grated parmesan. Mix well and leave to cool.

Slice the top off each of the zucchini. Scoop out the flesh with a spoon.

in Beef Bouillon

Mix the beaten eggs into the cooled stuffing and stir thoroughly to combine all the ingredients.

Fill each of the hollowed-out zucchini with meat stuffing. Heat the bouillon, to which the tomato concentrate has been added, in a pan. Stand the zucchini in the liquid, cover, and cook for 30 minutes.

During this time, cut the carrots, kohlrabi, peeled potatoes, and celery into large cubes. Shell the peas. Add the vegetables, with the bay leaf, salt, and pepper, to the pan. Simmer for 20 minutes. Eat piping hot.

Veal Escalope

Preparation time: *20 minutes*
Cooking time: *15 minutes*
Difficulty: ★

Serves 4

1	eggplant (aubergine)
6 tbsp/90 ml	olive oil
4	veal escalopes
½ cup/120 ml	white wine
4 slices	uncooked ham
2 tbsp/30 g	tomato sauce
8	basil leaves
4 slices	young pecorino cheese
	salt and pepper

For the garnish:

basil

Invaded many times in the course of their history, even as late as the 19th century Sardinians regarded the sea with suspicion. It was the sea that had brought Phoenicians, Carthaginians, Romans, Vandals, and Spanish invaders to their shores. Retreating to the mountainous regions inland, the local people survived by rearing animals. Many local dishes still feature ingredients reflecting this pastoral life. Veal escalope *alla barbaricina* is a dish typical of the Barbaria or Bargagia region, in the eastern part of the island. It is usually eaten at family meals on a Sunday or other festive occasion. A simple and delicious dish, it is ideal for serving to guests.

Veal escalopes are cut from the most tender parts of the animal, the cushion or the chump end. In this tasty recipe, the meat is covered with a slice of raw ham, a piece of fried eggplant, and some pecorino. About half of the total area of Sardinia is given over to animal husbandry. The local people are skilled cheese-makers, *pecorino sardo* being a particular favorite. Its mellow taste combines wonderfully with the meat in veal *alla barbaricina*. Made from pure ewe's milk, it is much loved by all Italians.

The tomato sauce served with the meat is a typically Sardinian touch. To make this, dice two tomatoes, half an onion, one stick of celery, and half a carrot. Heat a tablespoonful of olive oil in a pan, and brown one garlic clove and some chopped parsley. Add all the other vegetables together with a bay leaf, and cook for about half an hour. Season with salt and pepper, and sprinkle with basil. Blend the sauce in a food processor.

If you have not tried this deliciously flavored dish before, now is the time!

Wash the eggplant. Remove the stalk and cut the eggplant lengthwise into thin slices.

Heat 4 tbsp of olive oil, and gently fry the slices of eggplant. Pat them with a paper towel to remove any excess oil.

Heat the rest of the olive oil in an ovenproof dish. Add the veal escalopes and fry them for 2 minutes on either side.

Alla Barbaricina

Pour the white wine over the veal. Season with salt and pepper. Cook for about 4 minutes.

Place the slices of ham on the veal. Then pour over some tomato sauce and sprinkle with chopped basil.

Place the pieces of eggplant on the ham. Cover them with the pieces of cheese. Transfer the dish to the oven and cook at 400 °F/200 °C for 4–6 minutes. Serve the escalopes on plates with a drizzle of tomato sauce. Garnish with basil.

Lamb Fricassee with

Preparation time:	*45 minutes*
Cooking time:	*2 hours 15 minutes*
Difficulty:	★

Serves 4

1	shoulder of lamb weighing about 3 lb/1.4 kg
1¾ lb/800 g	green cabbage
7 oz/200 g	*figatellu* (Corsican sausage)
¼ cup/60 ml	olive oil
7 oz/200 g	large onions
2 tbsp/40 g	tomato concentrate
2 cups/500 ml	meat bouillon
2 cups/500 ml	Pietra beer
1	bouquet garni (bay and thyme)
	salt and freshly ground pepper

For the garnish:

½ bunch	parsley

Simple and filling, Corsican cooking is homely and rustic in character. Until relatively recently, people in the remoter villages, perched high in the mountains of this beautiful island, lived fiercely independent lives and were virtually self-sufficient in food, thanks to the local women's skilled use of available ingredients. This fricassee of lamb with cabbage and *figatellu* is an easily made dish that combines several traditional ingredients.

Sheep have grazed on Corsica since time immemorial, providing the basis for many delicious island dishes. The lambs are allowed to roam freely, grazing on the wild plants and herbs. Their relatively pale pink flesh has a very fine aroma and taste. For this recipe, Vincent Tabarani suggests using shoulder of lamb, or the collar.

This lamb fricassee with cabbage is similar to a hotpot, and typically eaten in winter. Cabbage seems to have arrived naturally in Europe about 4,000 years ago, quickly spreading throughout the continent during the Middle Ages. Used for medicinal purposes at first, it soon became a basic foodstuff.

Rich in vitamins A and C, green cabbage has a wrinkled appearance and mild taste. Choose a cabbage with firm, crisp leaves unmarked by blemishes or holes.

The flavor of the slow-cooked lamb is enhanced by the characteristic taste of *figatellu*. *Figatellu* is a typically Corsican sausage of pork liver that is still made in the traditional way in the Castagniccia region. Smoked for three or four days, the sausages can then be fried or broiled, or placed to dry in a well-ventilated place, after which they are eaten like salami. For this recipe, you could also use fatty smoked bacon or another type of smoked sausage.

Cut the meat off the bone and chop into equal-sized pieces.

Remove the outer leaves of the cabbage and discard. Detach all the leaves and chop and wash them.

Cut the figatellu *into large slices. Heat the olive oil and brown the pieces of* figatellu. *Set them aside. Brown the pieces of lamb in the same pan. Season with salt and pepper and set aside.*

Cabbage and Figatellu

Still using the same pan, soften the chopped onion. Add the cabbage and cook for about 10 minutes. Dilute the tomato concentrate with the meat bouillon. Pour it over the cabbage.

Add the Pietra beer and cook for about 30 minutes. Add the bouquet garni.

Return the pieces of lamb and figatellu *to the pan. Cover the pan and cook for about an hour and a half. Sprinkle with chopped parsley and serve.*

Knuckle of Pork with

Preparation time:	*30 minutes*
Cooking time:	*2 hours 40 minutes*
Soaking time for the garbanzo beans:	*overnight*
Difficulty:	★

Serves 4

2 cups/300 g	garbanzo beans (chickpeas)
2 lb/800 g	boned knuckle of pork
4 oz/100 g	onions
⅓ cup/80 ml	olive oil
4 oz/100 g	very ripe tomatoes
	salt and pepper

In the area around Mount Psiloriti (the ancient Mount Ida) in central Crete, marriage celebrations traditionally began the day before the wedding, when the parents of the bride-to-be would serve their future son-in-law a dish of pork and garbanzo beans, washed down with a good red wine. This custom is still observed, but the food offered today is more likely to be herb fritters or cakes.

Of the various cuts of pork, knuckle is the most suitable for this recipe. An alternative is chine, on or off the bone. The meat should be tender, without being too fatty. Bay leaf and cumin can be added to this delicious Cretan dish, greatly enhancing the flavors of the pork and tomatoes. The recipe also works well with lamb or beef shank.

Pork frequently features in Cretan cooking. In the old days, every family kept a pig, killing it just before Christmas. After the pre-Christmas fast, traditionally observed by Greek Catholics (or Melkites), the sudden abundance of meat and sausages was a cause of celebration. While some cuts of the meat were eaten fresh, the legs were smoked over the fireplace and other parts preserved in fat. These delicacies would then have been eaten throughout the year, on Sundays or other religious festivals.

Easy to store and highly nourishing, beans have always been an important part of the Cretan diet. Garbanzo beans are a particular favorite, and make a perfect accompaniment to cereals, fresh vegetables, and meat. They are enjoyed with tomato sauce, or in a mixture of flour and lemon juice. They also appear as *meze* accompanied by a glass of ouzo, puréed with olive oil and lemon, boiled in salads, or broiled and salted.

A garnish of chopped dill or parsley will add the finishing touch to this dish of pork and garbanzo beans.

Soak the garbanzo beans overnight in a bowl of cold water. The next day, drain them and blanch them rapidly in clean water. Drain again, then cover them with cold water and cook them for 2 hours (or until soft), removing any scum that comes to the top of the boiling water.

Cut the meat into cubes. Peel and chop the onions.

Brown the chopped onions in the olive oil in a saucepan for 5 minutes. Add the pieces of meat and brown them on all sides.

Garbanzo Beans Cretan Style

Cut the tomatoes in half and grate them on a vegetable grater over a bowl.

Pour the tomato pulp over the meat. Add salt and pepper. Cook for 20 minutes.

Now add the cooked, drained garbanzo beans. Continue to cook the meat and beans for about another 10 minutes, adding water if necessary. Serve hot.

Rabbit with Creamed Onions

Preparation time: *1 hour*
Cooking time: *1 hour 50 minutes*
Difficulty: ★★★

Serves 4

1	rabbit weighing 3 lb/1.5 kg
7/8 cup/100 g	flour
	olive oil
1	dried *ñora* pepper
1/2 bulb	garlic
4	large onions
1	bay leaf
1 sprig	thyme
3 or 4	chive stalks
3 or 4 sprigs	parsley
1 1/4 cups/300 ml	brandy
3	Mallorcan tomatoes
1 tbsp/15 g	paprika
12	large Sóller shrimp
	salt and pepper

For the *majado*:

1/2	rabbit liver
	olive oil
2 cloves	garlic
4 or 5 sprigs	flat-leaf parsley
1 sprig	fresh thyme

The Balearic Islands were conquered in 1229 by James I, king of Aragon and ally of the Catalan counts of Barcelona. The latter introduced their language and culture to the islands. Even today, the local cuisine and foodstuffs recall those of Barcelona. Chef Oscar Martínez Plaza, based in Palma de Mallorca, has created a dish combining Sóller shrimp with rabbit in a sauce of creamed onions.

Although the most commonly eaten meat on the Balearics is pork, rabbit-based dishes are much enjoyed. For a professional touch when presenting this dish, Oscar Martínez Plaza suggests pressing the meat of the rabbit thigh down the bone, to allow it to "sit" attractively on the plate. This recipe can also be made with skinned chicken thighs and drumsticks, which combine equally well with the flavor of shrimps.

The sauce in which the rabbit is cooked consists of vegetables and herbs. These give color and flavor to the meat. On Mallorca, *ñora* peppers and tomatoes are traditionally prepared in the same way: strung together, they are hung up on the walls of the local houses to dry in the sun. The *ñora* peppers become very dry and need to be rehydrated before use. Once soft, they should be cut open and scraped with a knife.

The magnificent natural harbor of Sóller is in north-west Mallorca. The fishermen of this quaint old seaside city, with its Art Deco architecture, devote half of their fleet to catching the shrimp that will put the finishing touches to this dish.

The usual method when making this recipe is to cook all the rabbit pieces in the oven. Oscar Martínez Plaza prefers to cook the saddle separately, so as to preserve its tenderness and delicate taste. When sliced up, it can be used to garnish the dish along with the fried onions and some chives.

Prepare the rabbit by jointing into legs, ribs, and saddle. Put the saddle to one side. Using a cleaver, chop the rest of the meat (on the bone) into smaller pieces. Coat these with seasoned flour and brown in the oil for 10 minutes. Remove the meat from the pan and set aside.

Put the ñora *pepper in water to soak. Brown the garlic in the oil used to cook the meat. Add the chopped onions (reserving half an onion) and a bouquet garni of bay, thyme, chives, and parsley. Add a third of the brandy and heat until the alcohol evaporates.*

Drain the softened ñora *pepper and scrape the flesh with a knife. Add it to the softened onions with 2 peeled and blended tomatoes and the paprika. Cook for a few minutes.*

and Sóller Shrimp

Add the pieces of fried rabbit to this mixture. Cover with water. Cook for 45 minutes until the rabbit is quite tender. In another pan, sauté the rabbit liver in oil. Grind it to make a majado *paste with garlic, parsley, and thyme. Add this to the rabbit.*

Peel the shrimp, and reserve the flesh. Sauté the shrimp heads and shells in oil for 5 minutes. Add 1 blended tomato and the remaining two thirds of the brandy. Cook for 10 minutes over a high heat. Strain this shrimp sauce through a sieve.

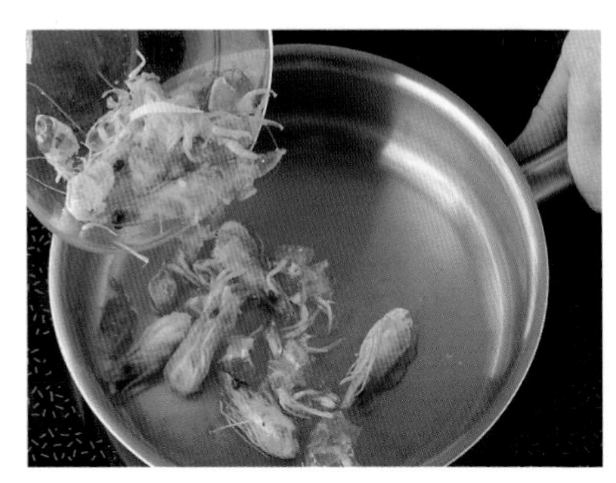

Slice the reserved half onion into thick rings. Blanch them, dip them in cold water, and dry them. Dip them in flour, and fry. Season the saddle of rabbit with salt and pepper, brush with oil, and cook it in a pan. Brown the shrimp meat in a separate pan. Serve everything piping hot with the sauce.

Rabbit

Preparation time: *50 minutes*
Cooking time: *40 minutes*
Difficulty: ★

Serves 4

1	rabbit weighing 2 lb/1 kg
2	carrots
1	celery heart
1 bunch	parsley
1 bunch	basil
2	onions
11 oz/300 g	tomatoes
4½ tbsp/70 ml	olive oil
1	small dried red pepper
1 knob	butter
3 tbsp/50 g	flour
2 oz/50 g	capers
5 oz/150 g	pitted green olives
7 tbsp/100 ml	red wine
7 tbsp/100 ml	white wine
	salt

For the garnish:

basil leaves

Rabbit *angelino*, a delicious family dish, is a particular specialty of chef Angelo La Spina's birthplace, Caltagirone. Famous for its pottery, this inland town retains its old Sicilian charm. Angelo La Spina has improved this traditional recipe with the addition of two typically Mediterranean ingredients: olives and capers.

Much enjoyed on Sicily, rabbit is normally broiled or stewed. At Easter, it is often served in rich, sweet-tasting sauce featuring pine nuts and raisins. Rabbit meat is firm and tasty, and combines well with other ingredients. Choose a rabbit that is not too long, with a rounded saddle, and a liver that is pale and free of blemishes. In season, select for preference the richer-flavored wild rabbit.

With its wonderful flavors, this dish is a good illustration of the subtlety of Sicilian cooking. Used in many of the island's specialties, Sicilian celery or *sedano* is chosen for its freshness and crisp texture. Cooked in combination with carrots and onions, also locally produced, celery is an essential ingredient. Available all year round, the exterior of the celery should be green, firm, and without black or brown marks.

Angelo La Spina's reworking of rabbit *angelino* is a treat. The highly prized Mediterranean olive finishes this typical southern Italian dish to perfection. Olive trees have grown in abundance on Sicily and the Aeolian Islands since Antiquity, particularly in the Biancavilla region near Catania. During the Roman Empire, olive oil began to be produced on a vast scale. The industry was controlled by the *arca olearia*, an official body that set the prices in this lucrative market.

Remove the rabbit liver and set aside. Divide the ribcage from the hindquarters at the point where the bottom of the ribs meets the saddle. Remove the legs and cut them into smaller pieces on the bone. Divide the saddle into pieces of equal size.

Prepare the vegetables. Peel the carrots and cut them into rounds. Wash and chop the celery, parsley, and basil.
Peel and chop the onions. Wash, peel, and mash the tomatoes (plunge them into just-boiled water first, to loosen the skins).

In a pan, heat 2 tbsp of the oil with the butter. Flour the pieces of rabbit meat, and fry them in the oil. Cook until golden, for about 10 minutes. Pat the pieces with a paper towel to remove excess oil and set aside.

Angelino

In the remaining oil, brown the chopped onions. Add the celery. Cook for about 5 minutes. Add the carrots, capers, parsley, and basil. Mix them all together. Sprinkle over the ground red pepper and add some salt. Add the tomatoes.

Mix the vegetables together. Add the sliced green olives. Cook for about 5 minutes.

Place the pieces of rabbit in an ovenproof dish. Cover them with the vegetable mixture. Add the red and white wine. Cook in the oven at 340 °F/170 °C for about 20 minutes. Serve the rabbit on plates accompanied by the vegetables and garnished with basil.

Free-Range Chicken with

Preparation time: *40 minutes*
Cooking time: *45 minutes*
Difficulty: ★

Serves 4

1	free-range chicken weighing 3 lb/ 1.4 kg
14 oz/400 g	tomatoes
1	onion
14 oz/400 g	red bell peppers
14 oz/400 g	green bell peppers
8 cloves	garlic
1/4 cup/60 ml	olive oil
1 bottle/750 ml	red wine
1	bouquet garni (thyme, bay leaf)
1/2 bunch	parsley
	salt and freshly ground pepper

Stews occupy an important place in Corsican cooking. This type of tasty home cooking uses nothing but locally produced ingredients. Chicken in red wine with peppers is a traditional dish, enjoyed throughout the island.

Chef Vincent Tabarani is an ardent promoter of the fine local produce marketed by the *Cucina Corsa* (Corsican Cooking) Association. Never one to compromise on ingredients, he insists on free-range chickens for this recipe, fed on wheat and other grains. These have a particularly tender and flavorsome meat. The city of Linguizetta, lying on the eastern plain to the south of Bastia, is famous for its excellent local poultry. As an alternative to chicken, this recipe can also be made with veal.

Wine is often combined with meat and game in Corsican cooking. For this recipe, Vincent Tabarani suggests a full-flavored and well-balanced, young Corsican wine.

Characteristic of the inland cooking of Corsica, this dish is filled with Mediterranean sunshine. Combined with olive oil, garlic, onion, and herbs, the chicken's flavors are enhanced by those of the tomatoes and bell peppers. Peppers, introduced originally from the New World, are now regarded as an intrinsic part of Mediterranean cuisine.

The flesh of red bell peppers has a soft and sweet flavor that is retained even when cooked. Green peppers, on the other hand, are picked before full maturity and so are sharper in taste and more crunchy. Often eaten raw in salads, sometimes peeled, the reds, greens, yellows, and oranges of bell peppers bring a brilliant splash of color to the stalls in Corsican markets. Choose peppers that are firm, smooth, and unmarked, with a stalk that is still green and rigid.

This inviting meal is suitable for any occasion.

To joint the chicken, first slit it down the back. Detach the legs. Detach the oyster and the tendons. Starting from the tip of the breastbone, cut through the ribs. Remove the breastbone and detach the wings (ask your butcher to do this for you if you prefer).

Peel the tomatoes by immersing them briefly in just-boiled water to loosen the skins. Crush them. Chop the onion. Remove the seeds from the red and green bell peppers and slice them into thin strips. Stab the garlic cloves with the point of a knife.

Heat the olive oil in a saucepan. Add the chicken pieces and cook for a few minutes. Season with salt and pepper.

Red Wine and Bell Peppers

Add the chopped onion to the chicken pieces. Mix together and brown for about 5 minutes.

Deglaze with the red wine. Put in the garlic cloves, still in their skin, and the bouquet garni. Add the crushed tomatoes. Cook over a high heat for about 20 minutes.

Add the bell peppers and check the seasoning. Cook gently for about 15 minutes. Sprinkle on the chopped parsley. Serve the chicken on plates with the pepper and wine sauce.

Lamb Stew with

Preparation time: *30 minutes*
Cooking time: *1 hour 20 minutes*
Difficulty: *★*

Serves 4

1¼ lb/600 g	fresh fava beans (broad beans)
2 lb/1 kg	leg of lamb
5 tbsp/75 ml	olive oil
2	onions
1 cup/250 ml	lamb bouillon
6	mint leaves
	salt and pepper

For the tomato sauce:

1 clove	garlic
1	onion
2 tbsp/30 ml	olive oil
7 oz/200 g	tomatoes
1	carrot
1 stick	celery
1	bay leaf
3	basil leaves
	salt and pepper

For the garnish:

mint leaves

No special event can be celebrated on Sardinia without a festive meal. Lamb stew with fresh fava beans is traditionally eaten on family occasions. Distinctive and full of flavor, this dish makes use of locally grown produce.

Once essentially a nation of sheep-farmers, the Sicilians' pastoral roots are reflected in their cuisine. In the past, when the men took the flocks to their summer grazing grounds, they lived on basic foods such as cheese, bread, and olive oil. If they ate meat at all, it was always roasted on a spit. On their return home, their wives would welcome them with a substantial and tasty stew.

The easily-made recipe given here uses leg of lamb, one of the best-flavored and favorite cuts. It is stewed with olive oil and onions, and given an extra freshness with the addition of mint. Believed to help digestion, this highly scented herb grows wild all over Sardinia.

Fava beans are central to this substantial stew. Fava beans originated in Persia, but have been eaten in the Mediterranean area since ancient times, and they are enjoyed for their unique and delicate flavor. Even when dried, fava beans are rich in proteins and vitamins. Fresh garden peas (from the same family of vegetables) can be used as an alternative if desired.

Pomodori (tomatoes) are essential for the rich color and flavor of this stew. Select those that are firm and plump with shiny skins and a uniform color. Grown in irrigated fields, and thriving in the island sunshine, Sardinian tomatoes are a favorite ingredient on the Italian mainland.

Shell the fresh fava beans and blanch them in a pan of salted water for about 4 minutes. Plunge them in a bowl of iced water and then drain.

Bone the leg of lamb and cut into equal-sized pieces (ask your butcher to do this if you prefer).

Brown the pieces of meat in very hot olive oil. Cook for a few minutes and then remove and set aside.

Fresh Fava Beans

In the same pan, brown the 2 chopped onions. Return the meat to the pan and add the bouillon. Bring to the boil and simmer for about 25 minutes.

For the sauce, brown the garlic and diced onion in the olive oil. Add the diced tomatoes, carrot, celery, and a bay leaf. Season with salt and pepper. Cook for 30 minutes. Add the basil. Blend the sauce in a food processor, then pour it over the lamb.

Season the lamb mixture. Add the chopped mint and the fava beans. Cook for about 10 minutes. Serve the stew on plates with a garnish of mint.

Bartolomé's Pig's

Preparation time:	*1 hour*
Cooking time:	*2 hours*
Refrigeration time for roulés:	*12 hours*
Difficulty:	★★

Serves 4

8	pig's trotters
2 cups/500 ml	meat bouillon
3	carrots
2	leeks
2	onions
2	bay leaves
2 sprigs	thyme
4 or 5 sprigs	parsley
1	*sobrasada* sausage
1 lb/500 g	cooked and shelled snails
1⅔ cups/400 ml	olive oil
	salt

The inhabitants of the Balearic Islands have enjoyed pork in all its forms since time immemorial. Pig's trotters are a popular dish on Mallorca, and are usually served in a vegetable and caper sauce. At his famous restaurant, *Xoriguer* in Palma, Bartolomé-Jaime Trias Luis has created a recipe for pig's trotters stuffed with *sobrasada*. These are then wrapped in green leek tops and served with snails in sauce.

Before cooking the pig's trotters, the remaining hairs on the pork skin should be removed by scraping with a razor. After long, slow cooking (for up to 3 hours) in vegetable bouillon, they are easily deboned and stuffed. *Sobrasada*, used as a stuffing in this recipe, is a large sausage typical of the Balearics. Made of pork, it is flavored and colored with paprika. The most famous type is made of meat from the local black pigs, reared in wooded areas of the islands.

Use leaves from large leeks to wrap the trotters. The leaves should be quickly blanched in boiling water, then plunged into cold water to preserve their bright green color. Place one stuffed pig's trotter on a leek leaf, trim the leaf's edges to fit, and roll up.

The sauce accompanying the pig's trotters is made with snails. Country people in the Balearics are very fond of these and, according to custom, go out on the second Monday in May every year to gather them. They are eaten with a variety of different sauces.

An original touch is given to this dish by the *sobrasada* juice. This is gently pressed out of the sausage meat with the back of a spoon during cooking, so that it blends with the cooking, turning it a bright red. The oil should not be too hot or it will burn the paprika, spoiling its taste.

Split the pig's trotters into two. Place them in a large pan with the bouillon, the roughly chopped carrots, 1 leek, the onions, some salt, and a bouquet garni (1 bay leaf, 1 sprig of thyme, and 2 sprigs of parsley). Bring the liquid to the boil, and cook for 1½ hours.

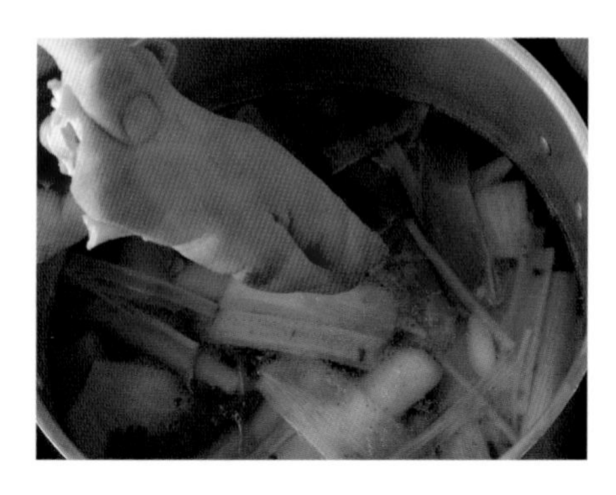

When the trotters are very tender but not falling apart, remove them from the pan, reserving the cooking liquid. Leave the trotters to cool and then remove the bones.

Cut the sobrasada *into strips 3 inches/7–8 cm long and ½ inch/1 cm wide. Use these to stuff the pig's trotters. Roll each one up in plastic wrap and refrigerate overnight.*

Trotter Roulés

Next day, slit the remaining leek lengthwise and wash. Blanch the leek and separate the leaves. Unwrap the pig's trotters and trim the edges neatly. Wrap each one in 2 or 3 rectangles of leek leaf. Slice into rounds slightly taller than they are wide.

Place the reserved cooking liquid in a pan with the snails. Add the meat bouillon and a bouquet garni (thyme, bay, and parsley). Bring the liquid to the boil and cook until a smooth sauce has been obtained.

Crumble the inside of a piece of sobrasada, *and cook it in hot oil until the oil becomes red. Strain the oil and reserve. Serve the pig's trotters garnished with a few snails, the snail sauce, some of the* sobrasada *juice, and pieces of fried sausage.*

Sautéed Rabbit in Garlic

Preparation time: *35 minutes*
Cooking time: *30 minutes*
Marinating time for rabbit: 6 hours
Difficulty: ★★

Serves 4

2	small rabbits
7 tbsp/100 ml	corn oil
6 cloves	garlic
3 sprigs	rosemary
3	bay leaves

$1^2/_3$ cups/400 ml	white wine
$1^1/_4$ cups/300 ml	beef bouillon
$1^1/_2$ cups/250 g	fresh shelled peas

For the marinade:

1	bay leaf
2 cups/500 ml	white wine
2 cloves	garlic
	salt and pepper

Every year since 1530, the Maltese have celebrated the festival of St Peter and St Paul on June 29. This religious holiday is also known as *Imnarja* (a word derived from the Latin *luminaria* or festival of lights). Mdina Cathedral, in the former capital city of Malta, is arrayed with illuminated decorations for the occasion. On the eve of the festival, on June 28, many families go to the Buskett gardens and the small woods surrounding Mdina, where they stay up all night and the following day, dancing, singing, and eating. This is traditionally an occasion for a *fenkata*: a meal based on rabbit, starting with pasta in rabbit sauce (*spaghetti bizzalza tal-fenek*), followed by sautéed rabbit with garlic and white wine (*fenek moqli*). The food will be washed down with plenty of the local wine.

Rabbit, *fenek*, is highly prized by Maltese food lovers. At one time, large numbers of rabbits lived wild in the countryside on the islands of Malta and Gozo. Today, most of the rabbits sold for eating are farmed chinchillas. The meat is served in many different ways: fried, stewed, in pies, or as a sauce for pasta.

The flavors of the marinade used in this recipe are taken up by the meat, making it tender and fragrant. When it is removed from the marinade, the meat should be carefully drained, and then dried with a cloth. This is to prevent the oil from spitting when the meat is browned.

When the meat is fully cooked in bouillon and wine (red or white), some cooks cover it with pastry to make a delicious pie.

This dish of sautéed rabbit goes well with French fries or just some crusty bread.

Chop the rabbit into small portions with a butcher's cleaver (ask your butcher to do this if you prefer).

For the marinade, arrange the meat in a shallow dish. Add the bay leaf, white wine, peeled garlic, salt, and pepper. Cover the meat with water. Place the dish in the refrigerator and leave the meat to marinate for 6 hours.

After 6 hours, drain the pieces of meat in a sieve. Then dry them well, rubbing them with a large cloth.

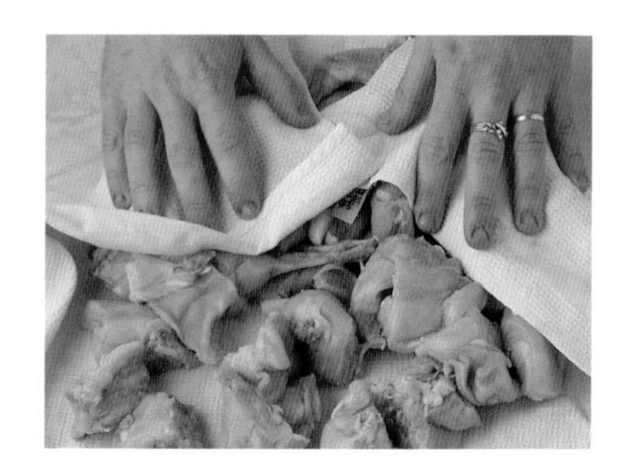

and White Wine

Heat 7 tbsp/100 ml of oil in a pan. When it is really hot, add the pieces of rabbit and turn them in the oil for 10 minutes until they are well browned. Pour off some of the oil. Add the chopped garlic and brown for 5 minutes.

Add the rosemary, bay leaves, and white wine to the rabbit in the pan. Cover and simmer for about 10 minutes, stirring from time to time until the wine has been absorbed.

Now add the beef bouillon and the peas. Continue cooking for about 5 minutes until the rabbit is tender, adding more bouillon if necessary.

Desserts & Pastries

Chestnut Flour

Preparation time: *35 minutes*
Cooking time: *30 minutes*
Difficulty: ★

Serves 4

1/3 cup/80 ml	olive oil
1/4 cup/30 g	wheat flour
3	eggs
1/2 cup/100g	superfine sugar
1/4 cup/60 ml	milk
1/2 envelope/2 1/2 tsp	baking powder
7 oz/200 g	chestnut flour

For the icing:

1/4 cup/60 ml	orange juice
4 1/2 oz/120 g	bitter chocolate
2 tbsp/30 ml	olive oil

This cake made with chestnut flour is a typically Corsican specialty. The sweet chestnut trees that grow on this beautiful Mediterranean island have been considered as a valuable source of food since ancient times, and chestnuts often sustained the population in times of famine. This substantial cake is easy to make. Iced with chocolate, it is generally eaten in fall and winter.

Like the wild pig, the chestnut is a symbol of Corsica. It is used in many dishes including the famous *pulenda*. In the old days, wedding banquets in the regions of Orezza, Cervione, and Alesani included 22 different dishes made with chestnut flour.

Castagniccia, Vincent Tabarani's home town, sits at an altitude of 1,500–3,000 feet/500–1,000 meters above sea level, surrounded by some 25,000 acres/10,000 hectares of chestnut trees. The nuts are harvested by hand and spread out on a *grata*, an arrangement of strips of wood placed a few inches apart, in the lofts of the local houses. Here, they are smoked and dried naturally in the heat from the *fucone* or hearth below. The nuts are then transported to the mill to be ground into flour.

Chestnut flour has a mild, toasted taste that is particularly sought after. An essential ingredient of this rich cake, it is generally available from December to May. Corsicans find that it will keep better if stored in a sealed glass jar.

Chocolate, the New World delicacy that has conquered the planet, came relatively late to Corsica. It is often melted in a bain-marie, over a low heat (do not exceed 120 °F/50 °C), but the method described here gives excellent results. Chocolate and chestnuts were, seemingly, made for each other, and the addition of orange juice gives extra zest to the icing of this delicious cake.

Lightly oil and flour the baking pan. Place it in the refrigerator while preparing the cake mixture. Place the egg yolks and sugar in a bowl. Beat until a pale cream.

Gradually add the remaining olive oil to the mixture. Beat with a whisk. Add the milk.

Whip the egg whites until stiff. Gently fold them into the eggs and sugar mixture.

Cake

Sieve together the baking powder and chestnut flour. Add them carefully to the bowl and mix in with a whisk.

Preheat the oven to 300 °F/150 °C. Pour the cake mixture into the prepared baking pan. Cook in the oven for 30 minutes. When cooked, allow the cake to cool slightly, then turn it out from the baking pan.

Bring the orange juice to the boil with 2 tbsp of water. Remove from the heat and add the chocolate, broken into pieces. Blend in the chocolate as it melts. Gradually mix in the olive oil. Allow to cool slightly. Smooth the chocolate icing over the chestnut flour cake and serve.

Blancmange with

Preparation time: *40 minutes*
Cooking time: *40 minutes*
Refrigerating time for the blancmange: *6 hours*
Difficulty: ★

Serves 4

2	lemons
2/3 cup/75 g	ground almonds
1/3 cup/70 g	superfine sugar
1/2 cup/45 g	cornstarch

For the lemon sauce:

3	lemons
4 1/2 oz/120 g	lump sugar
3	eggs
5/8 stick/70 g	butter

For the garnish:

sprigs of mint
orange peel
ground cinnamon

The recipe for blancmange is very ancient. Made of almonds, it is particularly popular in the Modica region of Sicily where it is traditionally eaten for breakfast or in the afternoon during the long, hot summer.

The origins of this dish can be traced back to the Middle Ages. On Sicily, it was customary to prepare a nourishing, salted dish of the same name for the sick, and for young mothers. This consisted of almond milk to which ground chicken and spices were added. In the course of time, this *biancomangiare* (meaning literally "white" and "eat") evolved into a dessert.

This delicious recipe is very easy to make. The combination of lemons, oranges, and almonds is typically Sicilian. Almonds are used in the preparation of many local sweet specialties including marzipan, *torrone* (a kind of nougat), and *pasta reale* (a kind of cake). In early spring, the Agrigento plain and the area around Siracusa are a mass of almond blossom.

The blancmange is traditionally poured into molds in the shape of characters from folklore. In Sicilian homes, the dessert is often served in a lemon leaf, inspiring Giuseppe Barone to add a lemon sauce to his recipe.

Famous throughout the world, many different varieties of lemons are grown on Sicily, such as *verdello*, *monachello*, and *femminello*. Lemons probably originated in India, and were introduced to Sicily by the Arabs in the early Middle Ages, where they quickly adapted to their new home thanks to an ingenious system of irrigation. For the sauce used here, the lemon skins should first be thoroughly washed in warm water.

This refreshing, refined dessert is guaranteed to please.

Wash 2 lemons. Using a sharp knife, cut away the zest in pieces, leaving the pith intact. Blanch the pieces of zest in 2 cups/500 ml water for about 2 minutes. Remove the zest and reserve the water.

Place the ground almonds in a piece of fine muslin and make into a bag. Immerse it in the reserved water used to cook the lemon zest and squeeze the bag to press out the almond "milk." Strain and reserve the resulting liquid.

Add the sugar and cornstarch to the almond milk. Warm very gently over a low heat, stirring the mixture with a whisk until it thickens into a cream.

Lemon Sauce

Ladle the mixture into molds that have first been slightly wetted. Refrigerate the blancmanges for 6 hours.

To make the sauce, carefully wash the 3 remaining lemons, remove the zest using the sugar lumps (or a special lemon zester, if you have one), and extract their juice.

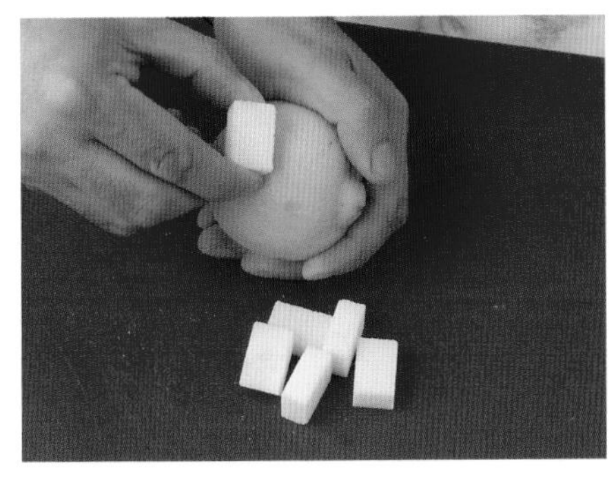

Break the eggs into a saucepan and add the sugar, butter, and lemon juice. Cook the sauce in a bain-marie, beating constantly. Turn the blancmanges out of their molds. Pour some lemon sauce around each one. Garnish with mint, fine strips of orange peel, and cinnamon.

Sicilian

Preparation time: *50 minutes*
Cooking time: *15 minutes*
Refrigeration time for the pastry: *2 hours*
Difficulty: ★★

Serves 8

½ tsp/5 g	shortening
	vegetable oil for frying
½ cup/50 g	flour

For the pastry:

4⅖ cups/500 g	flour
⅓ cup/70 g	superfine sugar
⅝ stick/70 g	shortening
	salt
1	egg
⅔ cup/150 ml	red wine

For the filling:

1 lb/500 g	ricotta
1⅓ cups/300 g	superfine sugar
½	cinnamon stick
¼ cup/25 g	chocolate chips
¼ cup/25 g	chopped almonds

For the garnish:

confectioners' sugar

No less famous than the delicious and festive Sicilian *cassata*, *cannoli siciliani* are long rolls of fried pastry filled with sweetened ricotta. Traditionally associated with the *carnevale* festivities immediately before the Lent fast, this dessert is now eaten at any time of year and is frequently offered to guests.

Sicilian cuisine is a mixture of many ethnic influences. The Arabs, who occupied the island from the 9th to the 11th centuries, greatly enriched the local dishes. *Cannoli*, now internationally famous, seem likely to date from this period. The fillings used vary from town to town, and may include dried fruits, pistachio nuts, or *crème pâtissière* (confectioners' custard). In Palermo, the filling contains pumpkin flesh and oranges.

Every Sicilian family has its own recipe, with even the ingredients of the pastry varying from one cook to the next. Some people color the pastry with chocolate while others, like Angelo La Spina, use red wine. The shortening is sometimes replaced by butter. One thing that does not vary, however, is the shape of the *cannoli*, traditionally achieved by rolling circular pieces of pastry (about 5 inches/12 cm across) around a section of bamboo. The pastry rolls are then deep-fried in oil.

The creamy filling used here consists of ricotta cheese (the Italian word *ricotta* means "recooked"). This famous Sicilian cheese is made of the whey from cow's, ewe's, or goat's milk, and has a mild, slightly tangy taste. Flavored in this recipe with a hint of cinnamon, its smooth texture contrasts deliciously with the crunchiness of the pastry and chopped almonds.

This delicate dessert is a perfect introduction to the subtleties of Sicilian cuisine.

For the pastry, heap the flour on the working surface, make a well in the middle and add the sugar, shortening, salt, and egg. Mix everything together, then slowly incorporate the red wine. Knead the mixture until a firm paste is obtained. Leave to rest for 2 hours.

For the filling, place the ricotta in a bowl, mix it to a smooth consistency and add the sugar. Grate the cinnamon stick (use a nutmeg grater for this, or use a ½ tsp of powdered cinnamon) and add, together with the chocolate chips. Mix well.

Toast the chopped almonds and add them to the ricotta mixture (keep a little back to garnish). Mix carefully with a spatula.

Cannoli

Knead the pastry into a ball. Cut into equal-sized pieces. Roll each piece out into a circle and wrap the circle around a cook-proof cylindrical mold greased with shortening.

Heat the vegetable oil. Immerse the cannoli *one by one, still wrapped around the cylinders. Fry until golden, then drain on a piece of paper towel and leave to cool. Carefully slide off the mold.*

Using a spatula, carefully fill the cannoli *with the ricotta mixture. Garnish them with confectioners' sugar, and dip the ends in the remaining toasted almonds. Serve.*

Rice Crispelle

Preparation time:	*15 minutes*
Cooking time:	*40 minutes*
Proving time for rice:	*3 hours*
Difficulty:	★

Serves 4

2 cups/500 ml	whole milk
1¼ cups/250 g	white rice
1	orange
2 cups/220 g	flour
½ oz/10 g	fresh brewer's yeast
	vegetable oil for frying
5 tbsp/150 g	carob or other honey

For the garnish (optional):

pinch	powdered cinnamon

In Sicilian cooking, the term *crispelle* describes any of the delicious fried specialties eaten during Carnival. Very popular today, these fritters were originally eaten only by the Sicilian nobility.

Before the unification of Italy, primogeniture was strictly observed on Sicily. The younger sons of wealthy families had to make their own way in the world and, since paid work was inconceivable, they often took holy orders. Wanting to continue to live in the manner to which they had been accustomed, they engaged famous chefs from France to cook for their monasteries.

The French chefs' style of cooking—known as *monzu*, a corruption of the title *Monsieur*, by which they would have been addressed—was famously elaborate and opulent. It is remembered in a number of Sicilian specialties, including *timballo di maccheroni* (macaroni with a cheese sauce and pastry crust), and *farsumagru*, a kind of stuffed, rolled veal. Among the desserts introduced by the French chefs are the rice *crispelle* described here.

These easily-made desserts are a real treat. The rice, the main ingredient of the recipe, should be washed before use. It is cooked for about 20 minutes in milk and water, and then mixed together with the other ingredients, one of which is yeast. It is important to allow the mixture to prove for at least 3 hours before making the fritters.

Crisp outside, with a soft interior, the *crispelle* are coated with delicately flavored carob honey. Growing wild on Sicily, the carob tree has pod-like fruit that grow to a length of 12 inches/30 cm. These contain a nutritious pulp that is both refreshing and rich in sugar. The carob pods are generally crushed and used to make a delicious jam and a liqueur. Other honeys may also be used.

Pour the whole milk into a pan with 2 cups/500 ml of water. Bring to the boil and add the washed rice. Cook the rice for about 20 minutes. Leave to cool.

Thoroughly wash the orange, then grate the peel.

Transfer the rice to a bowl. Add most of the flour (leaving a little for flouring the fritters), the yeast, and the grated orange peel. Mix well. Leave to prove for at least 3 hours. If using active dry yeast, follow maker's instructions.

with Honey

Flour the working surface with the remaining flour. Place spoonfuls of the mixture on the flour, and shape into fritters, coating them with flour.

Heat the frying oil. Immerse the fritters and fry until golden. Remove and drain on a piece of paper towel.

Warm the honey in a pan to soften. Dip the fritters in the honey, drain, and serve.

Carob & Hazelnut Cake with

Preparation time: *1 hour*
Cooking time: *1 hour*
Difficulty: ★★

Serves 4

For the almond mousse:

2 cups/500 ml	milk
1 cup/150 g	blanched almonds
3 sheets	gelatin
½ cup/100 g	sugar
5½ oz/150 g	egg yolks
4 oz/100 g	egg whites
1¼ cups/300 ml	crème fraîche, whipped to the soft peak stage

For the cake:

6	eggs
1 cup/100 g	ground hazelnuts
½ cup/75 g	chopped hazelnuts
2 tbsp/30 g	carob powder
1	orange
1	lemon
3 tbsp/45 g	sugar

For the Palo sauce:

¼ cup/50 g	brown sugar
⅘ cup/200 ml	Palo liqueur
1 cup/250 ml	milk
3½ tbsp/50 ml	crème fraîche

For the garnish (optional):

fresh raspberries
mint leaves
chocolate leaves

Bartolomé-Jaime Trias Luis and his colleague Oscar Martínez Plaza serve this delicious combination of hazelnut and carob cake, almond mousse, and a liqueur sauce, at their restaurant in Palma de Mallorca.

The rich but light cake is inspired by a traditional hazelnut mixture, but with the addition of carob powder. Carob pods, which resemble black fava bean pods, contain flat, sugar-rich seeds. Low in fat and containing no caffeine or theobromine, they are sold in powdered form as a substitute for chocolate and coffee. Chocolate-lovers may wish to add some cocoa to the carob powder, or some chocolate chips.

The mousse accompanying the cake is based on almond milk. Blend the almonds with the milk until a smooth liquid is obtained, then strain it. The result will be a smooth, custard-like sauce. When whipping the egg whites, do not add the sugar until they are beginning to stiffen. Then continue beating until the mixture is thick, smooth, and shiny, when it will cling to the whisk.

Complementing this duo of Balearic delights is a delicious caramel sauce made of milk, cream, and Palo liqueur. Palo is popular with the older generation, who can be seen drinking it at any time of day, served cold with ice, soda, or sparkling water. It is black in color, and made of a mixture of aniseed brandy, licorice, herb roots, and caramel. If Palo is unavailable, kahlua (although quite different in taste) would make an acceptable alternative.

To serve this dessert, arrange two rectangular slices of cake on each plate with, next to them, two little pools of Palo cream, decorated with raspberry halves and mint leaves. Place a spoonful of almond mousse and a chocolate leaf on top of each piece of cake.

To make the almond mousse, place the milk and almonds in the bowl of a food processor. Blend well, then strain the mixture. Soften the gelatin in a bowl of cold water.

Add the sugar to the almond milk and heat. Beat the egg yolks in a bowl, then pour the sugar and almond mixture over them and mix well. Return the mixture to the saucepan and cook gently until it thickens. Add the gelatin, beating it into the mixture as it dissolves. Cool.

Whip the egg whites until stiff. Fold them into the cool almond cream. Allow to rest for 30 minutes, then fold in the whipped crème fraîche. Place in a refrigerator.

Almond Mousse & Palo Sauce

For the cake, separate 6 eggs. To the yolks, add the ground and chopped hazelnuts, the carob powder, and the zest of the orange and lemon. Mix these together in a food processor.

Beat the six egg whites with the sugar until they form stiff peaks. Fold into the cake mixture. Spread the mixture into a baking pan lined with waxed paper, pressing it down very gently. Cook for 20 minutes in a medium oven (350 °F/180 °C).

For the Palo sauce, heat the sugar with a little water until it caramelizes. Cool it by adding the Palo liqueur, allow it to reduce a little, then add the milk and cream. Bring the sauce to the boil, then cool. Serve the cake topped with a spoonful of almond mousse, surrounded by Palo sauce.

Fiadone

Preparation time:	*15 minutes*
Cooking time:	*25 minutes*
Difficulty:	★

Serves 4

1 lb/500 g	*brocciu* (Corsican soft cheese)
1	lemon
1 1/3 cups/300 g	superfine sugar
6	eggs
2 tsp/10 ml	eau-de-vie
1 tbsp/10 g	butter

A favorite cake on Corsica, *fiadone* has an ancient history. Made of *brocciu* and eggs, it is often made for the festivities associated with religious ceremonies such as baptism, a young person's first communion, and marriage. Despite the small number of ingredients, this typically Corsican specialty is truly delicious.

Fiadone is very easy to make. The main thing to remember is that the mixture should fill the baking pan to a depth of 1 5/8 inches/4 cm. Perhaps the most famous of Corsican cheeses, *brocciu* has been awarded a coveted *appellation d'origine contrôlée*, guaranteeing its authenticity and quality. Made since time immemorial from the whey milk of ewes or goats, whole milk, and salt, it has a very mild flavor. An indispensable ingredient in many local dishes, it is a proud reminder of the island's pastoral traditions.

A reference to the farming of animals on Corsica is found as early as the 2nd century BC in the *Rise of the Roman Republic* by the Greek historian Polybius: "The impression that all the animals on the island are wild arises from the following cause. The island is thickly wooded and the countryside so rocky and precipitous that it is impossible for the shepherds to follow their flocks and herds about as they graze. So whenever they wish to collect them they take up position in some convenient place; from there they summon them by horn, and all the animals respond without fail to the instrument which they recognize." (Book XII, p. 430 in the translation by Ian Scott-Kilvert, Penguin Classics, 1979.)

The *fiadone* is flavored with a little local eau-de-vie (clear fruit brandy) and grated lemon peel. Known as a good source of vitamin C, lemons are grown in large numbers on the island. Choose unwaxed lemons if possible; otherwise, scrub the peel thoroughly in hot water. Firm, unblemished lemons will keep in the salad compartment of the refrigerator for at least two weeks.

Place the brocciu *in a bowl and mash it with a whisk or fork.*

Wash the lemon thoroughly, then grate the peel.

Pour the sugar into the bowl of brocciu*. Add the eggs. Mix together until smooth and evenly textured.*

Add the lemon peel, then the eau-de-vie. Mix thoroughly.

Using a brush, lightly grease the baking pan with softened butter.

Pour the brocciu *mixture into the pan. Cook in a medium oven (350 °F/180 °C) for about 25 minutes. When baked, turn the cake out of the pan and serve warm or cold.*

Gelat

Preparation time:	*30 minutes*
Cooking time for custard:	*25 minutes*
Baking time for cookies:	*15 minutes*
Preparation of ice cream:	*20 minutes*
Difficulty:	★★

Serves 4

For the parmesan ice cream:

2 cups/500 ml	milk
1 stick	cinnamon
	zest of 1 orange
	zest of 1 lemon
1	vanilla pod
3/8 cup/80 g	sugar
3 tbsp/100 g	honey
2 oz/50 g	grated parmesan
6	eggs
7 tbsp/100 ml	light cream

For the "village" cookies:

4	eggs
1 cup/250 g	sugar
1 tbsp/15 g	aniseed seeds
	grated zest of 1 orange
1	vanilla pod
6 cups/550 g	cake flour (self-raising)

For the garnish (optional):

	candied orange peel
	ground cinnamon

Gelat bil-gobon is said to have been invented in the mid-18th century by a Maltese chef called Michele Marceca. This curious recipe combines a spiced custard, or *crème anglaise*, with fresh cream and parmesan cheese. Iced desserts were very popular in the 18th century, when the Knights of St John still governed the island. The Knights had blocks of ice brought from the slopes of Mount Etna on nearby Sicily. The blocks were stored in cool caves or ice-houses, wrapped in straw.

The parmesan cheese incorporated into the mixture in the final stages is still made only in Parma, on the Italian mainland. Malta produces only small goat's-milk cheeses, and a kind of ricotta.

To accompany the ice cream, Michael Cauchi suggests the traditional *biskuttini tar-rahal* ("village" cookies). This simple recipe is often prepared for celebrations and ceremonies. The cookies can be flavored with a variety of ingredients, according to preference, for example: grated orange or lemon peel, vanilla seeds, ground cinnamon, cloves, aniseed, or anisette.

The shape of the cookie is left to the imagination of the cook: long sticks, small round balls, small domes shaped with an icing bag, or sausage-shaped cookies made using two spoons. For the latter, dip two spoons into hot water, take a spoonful of cookie mixture and shape it by rolling from one spoon to the other. To cook, place the shaped mixture on a baking sheet covered with waxed or silicone paper and bake in a hot oven.

The cookies can be eaten as a side accompaniment or, for special occasions, chopped and then crumbled into the base of individual ice cream dishes. Spoon the ice cream over them, and press down well. To garnish, sprinkle with ground cinnamon, and decorate with strips of candied orange peel.

Begin by making the ice cream. For this, heat the milk in a saucepan. Add the cinnamon, a few strips of orange and lemon peel, and the vanilla seeds. Let these infuse for 10 minutes over a low heat.

Add the sugar and honey to the spiced milk. Mix and then strain the mixture into another saucepan. Add the grated parmesan, stirring for about 5 minutes over the heat until it has dissolved.

Beat 6 egg yolks in a bowl. Dilute them with some of the spiced milk, then add the contents of the bowl to the saucepan. Cook the mixture gently for about 10 minutes until a smooth custard has been obtained.

Bil-Gobon

When the custard is ready, pour in the fresh cream. Allow the mixture to cool, then place it in an ice-cream maker. When the ice-cream is ready, transfer it from the ice-cream maker to a container, and place it in the freezer until required.

For the cookies, beat the egg whites with the sugar until stiff peaks form. Add the aniseed, grated orange peel, and vanilla pods, together with the beaten egg yolks and most of the flour (reserving a little to flour the work surface). Mix gently until a smooth paste is obtained.

Flour the work surface. Using two spoons, shape the mixture into cookies and arrange them on a baking sheet. Cook for 15 minutes in a hot oven (400 °F/200 °C). Arrange the ice cream and cookies in glasses to serve.

Kalitsounia

Preparation time: *40 minutes*
Cooking time: *30 minutes*
Resting time for pastry: *30 minutes*
Difficulty: ★★

Serves 6

For the pastry:

5¼ cups/600 g	flour
1 tsp/5 g	dried yeast
⅔ cup/150 g	sugar
⅝ stick/75 g	butter
⅓ cup/80 ml	olive oil
3	eggs

For the filling:

2¼ lb/1 kg	fresh *myzithra* cheese
1	egg
⅔ cup/150 g	sugar
1 tsp/5 g	ground cinnamon

These delicious *kalitsounia* are offered to guests at Eastertime on Crete, and are traditionally prepared on the morning of the Thursday before Good Friday. The little tarts with a filling of sweetened cheese are often made at home, but they are also sold by local bakers and, increasingly, manufactured in larger quantities.

Kalitsounia are usually shaped like small, pointed crowns. They are also known as *lychnarakia* ("little oil lamps") due to their resemblance to ancient, open oil burners. *Kalitsounia* can also be triangular or square. Those made in Heraklion have a pastry lid. In the past, large square *kalitsounia* were cooked slowly in wood-fired ovens, giving them a unique flavor.

In this recipe the pastry is made with both butter and oil, but not all recipes for *kalitsounia* include butter. Live yeast and milk are sometimes used, making the cakes puff up like small brioches. Whichever recipe is preferred, perfect flavorings for the pastry are ground coriander and mastic.

The basis of the filling is fresh, mild *myzithra* cheese. Good substitutes are fresh ewe's-milk cheeses such as *brousse* or ricotta. The cheese can be flavored to taste with vanilla sugar, cinnamon, fresh mint, or honey.

When the *kalitsounia* are ready, Michalis Markakis brushes them with egg yolk and sprinkles them with cinnamon. Cinnamon tends to go black when baked, so you might prefer to add this after cooking.

The *kalitsounia* will keep fresh for at least two weeks. On Crete, they are often stored in boxes with layers of dried orange or lemon leaves above and below. This gives the cakes a subtle aroma of citrus fruits, and the leaves also make attractive decorations when serving.

First make the pastry. Place the flour in a bowl, making a well in the center. To this add the yeast, sugar, slices of butter, olive oil, and 3 eggs.

Mix the ingredients together with the tips of the fingers until they form a smooth, well-mixed pastry. Squeeze it all together to make a ball and leave to rest for 30 minutes.

Roll out the pastry on a floured surface until it is ¼ inch/0.5 cm thick. With a 3½ inch/9 cm tart cutter, cut out pastry circles. Preheat the oven to 320 °F/160 °C.

To make the filling, put the myzithra *cheese into a bowl with the egg, sugar, and ground cinnamon. Mix well.*

Put a teaspoonful of filling in the center of each piece of pastry.

Pinch the edges of the pastry together around the filling, giving the cakes a crown-like appearance. Arrange them on a baking sheet covered with buttered silicone (or waxed) paper. Brush them with egg yolk and cook for 30 minutes at 320–340 °F/160–170 °C.

Maltese

Preparation time: *40 minutes*
Cooking time: *40 minutes*
Marinating time for dates: *overnight*
Pastry resting time: *1 hour*
Difficulty: ★★

Serves 4

For the pastry:

$^2/_3$ cup/150 ml	orange juice
$^1/_2$ cup/100 g	sugar
7 tbsp/100 ml	olive oil
$4^2/_5$ cups/500 g	flour

For the date filling:

2 lb/1 kg	soft dates
4 tbsp/60 ml	Maltese anisette
1 tsp/5 g	ground cinnamon
1 tsp/5 g	ground cloves
2 tbsp/30 ml	orange flower (or rose) water
1	orange
1	lemon
	oil for frying

In the summer on Malta, anyone walking by the sea at Msida, to the south-west of Valletta, will not fail to notice a wonderful scent of hot oil and aniseed. It is a sure sign that a stall has been set up nearby, selling *mqaret*, delicious Maltese fried cakes filled with a paste of dates flavored with spices and aniseed. The same tempting delicacy is sold by street sellers near the City Gate, the main entrance to Valletta, the capital of Malta. Known for centuries, this delicacy appears today not only at village festivals in the wintertime, but also on the menu in some of the best restaurants on Malta.

As can be seen from their name, *mqaret* are similar to the Algerian and Tunisian *makroud*. Date palms do not grow on Malta, so the dates used are imported from Tunisia.

Depending on the recipe, the pastry is made with oil, shortening, or butter. Butter gives a firmer texture, making the pastry easier to roll out. The pastry needs to rest for one hour before being rolled out very thinly with a rolling pin or, preferably, in a pasta maker.

Michael Cauchi suggests flavoring the date filling with Maltese anisette. This aniseed and herb-flavored liquor is generally drunk well chilled with a mixer (water, lemonade, or orange or pineapple juice).

Citrus fruits are cultivated on Malta, including one of the most delicious oranges in the world, the celebrated "Maltese" or "blood" orange. It comes as no surprise, therefore, that orange juice is used here for the pastry, and orange flower water for the filling.

Mqaret are cut into lozenges and fried or baked. Eaten hot, they melt deliciously in the mouth, but they may also be eaten warm or cold.

Blend the pitted dates in a food processor, then cook them for 30 minutes in the water and anisette. Leave to marinate overnight. To make the pastry, put the orange juice and sugar in a bowl. Mix them together, then add the oil.

Add the flour to the mixture, kneading well until a smooth dough is obtained. Form this into a ball, cover with plastic wrap, and leave to rest for 1 hour.

Now prepare the filling. Mix together the marinated dates, cinnamon, ground cloves, orange flower water, one tbsp of chopped orange peel, and one tbsp of chopped lemon peel.

Mqaret

Roll out the pastry and cut it into large rectangles of approximately 8 inches/20 cm by 4 inches/8–10 cm. Place a line of filling down one side of each rectangle. Using a brush, make the other edge of the pastry slightly wet.

Roll the pastry around the filling. Flatten the long roll and cut it obliquely at intervals of about 1 inch/3 cm to obtain the typical lozenge-shaped mqaret.

Deep-fry the mqaret *in oil heated to 350 °F/180 °C until golden. Drain on a paper towel. Eat while still hot.*

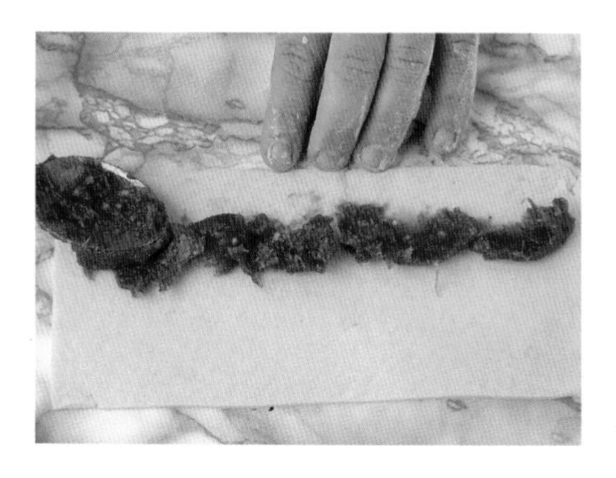

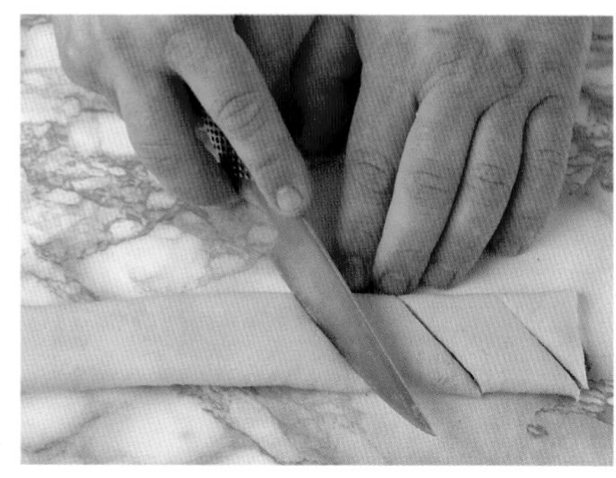

Oreillettes Filled with

Preparation time:	*1 hour*
Cooking time:	*15 minutes*
Refrigeration time for dough:	*1 hour*
Proving time:	*40 minutes*
Difficulty:	★

Serves 4

7/8 cup/100 g	flour
4 cups/1 liter	olive oil for frying
2/5 cup/100 g	superfine sugar

For the dough:

4 2/5 cups/500 g	flour
2 envelopes/10 g	dried yeast
3	eggs
1 stick/100 g	shortening
7 oz/200 g	condensed milk
	grated peel of ½ lemon
2 tbsp/30 ml	pastis
	salt

For the filling:

5 oz/150 g	*brocciu* (Corsican cheese)
	grated zest of ½ orange
3/8 cup/50 g	confectioners' sugar
2 tbsp/30 ml	grape eau-de-vie
1	egg

Oreillettes (meaning "little ears") are synonymous on Corsica with special occasions. They are made for marriages, baptisms, and first communions. Fried and sugared, they are very popular, and a big pile is always placed on the table for family and friends. They can be soft or crispy, according to taste.

The dough for *oreillettes* is simple to prepare, and can be made the day before it is needed. Made from flour, yeast, lemon, salt, and eggs, it also includes a little pastis. This aniseed and herb flavored aperitif originates from Marseilles in south-eastern France, and is drunk diluted with water, when its gold color turns a pale, opaque eau-de-nil.

Traditionally, these Corsican doughnuts were served without filling. Vincent Tabarani, who learned the recipe from his mother, suggests adding a sweetened cheese filling made with *brocciu*, to make them even more special.

Brocciu is a traditional Corsican cheese made by shepherds since ancient times. To prepare it, the whey of ewe's or goat's milk is heated over a wood fire in a large metal pot. The mixture is cooled, and the whole milk and salt are added. The shepherds then skim off the solidifying cheese that forms on the surface of the milk, and pack it into small round baskets woven from reeds.

The resulting cheese is very fresh and very mild. It is used in cooking for both sweet and savory dishes. Ricotta, very similar in taste, can be used in its place.

The cheese filling is flavored with *aquavita*, an eau-de-vie (clear brandy) made from grapes. This is one of many liqueurs of this type made on Corsica, from a variety of different fruits including blueberries, grapes, oranges, and arbutus berries. A small glass of *aquavita* is offered to guests throughout the island, as a mark of hospitality.

For the dough, heap the flour and yeast on a work surface. Make a well in the center. Into this put the egg yolks, melted shortening, condensed milk, grated lemon peel, stiffly beaten egg whites, pastis, and salt. Incorporate the ingredients and knead to make dough. Refrigerate for 1 hour.

For the filling, put the brocciu *into a bowl with the orange zests, confectioners' sugar, and eau-de-vie. Mash these together, then add the egg, mixing thoroughly with a whisk.*

Cut the ball of dough into two pieces. Flour the work surface and roll out the dough balls to a thickness of 1/8 inch/2 mm.

Aquavita-Flavored Brocciu

Cut out circles of dough using a 4½ inch/10–12 cm cutter.

Place a little filling on each circle of dough. Slightly dampen the edges of the dough with a brush dipped in water.

Fold the dough circles to make semicircular parcels. Place these on a cloth for about 40 minutes to prove, then fry them in hot olive oil and drain on paper towels. Roll them in sugar and serve.

Patouda

Preparation time: *40 minutes*
Cooking time: *40 minutes*
Infusion time for the ash: *1 hour*
Difficulty: ★★

Serves 6

For the pastry:

7 oz/200 g	*alousia* (wood ash)
3 lb/1.5 kg	flour
½ tsp/2½ g	baking powder
2 tsp/10 ml	*tsikoudia* (eau-de-vie)
3 cups/750 ml	olive oil

For the filling:

1 lb/500 g	chopped almonds
1 lb/500 g	shelled walnuts
10 level tbsp/300 g	thyme honey
7/8 cup/200 g	superfine sugar
pinch	ground cinnamon
pinch	ground cloves
1 tsp/5 ml	nutmeg

For the decoration:

confectioners' sugar

Patouda are small semicircular pastries filled with dried fruits and honey, eaten particularly at Christmas. This recipe is from Sitia, in the east of Crete. Some writers have suggested that it is descended from *gastrin*, cakes made with nuts, almonds, poppy seeds, and honey, described by Atheneus in his *Banquet of the Sophists*, dating from the 2nd or 3rd century AD.

The pastry used for *patouda* contains two rather unusual ingredients. One is wood ash, used at the outset as an infusion. Packets of *alousia*, finely ground ash from the wood of pine or olive trees, are easily found in shops on Crete. The liquid in which the ash has been infused is used to make the pastry lighter (when mixed with water, the ash releases soda). The action of the ash infusion is reinforced by the second unusual ingredient, a raising agent known in Greek as *ammonia*. This should not be confused with the toxic chemical of the same name in English. These two ingredients can be replaced with the same quantities of baking powder. To prepare the infusion, tie the ash in a piece of muslin and pour boiling water over it. Remove the sieve with the bag of ash and leave the water to infuse for one hour, allowing any traces of ash to fall to the bottom of the bowl.

When the spiced syrup used for the filling has come to the boil, a scum will form on the surface. This should be carefully removed before pouring the syrup into the nut mixture. Some people add ground raisins to the nuts.

There are two ways of making the *patouda*: either roll out the pastry and cut it into small circles, or make small balls of pastry and roll each one out separately. Place some filling in each piece of pastry and fold the *patouda* into semicircles, sealing the edges with cold water or, preferably, orange flower water or rose water.

For the pastry, place the wood ash in a piece of cloth. Tie it into a bag and place it in a sieve over a bowl. Pour over 4/5 cup/200 ml boiling water. Leave to rest for 1 hour. Put the flour, baking powder, ash infusion, eau-de-vie (clear brandy), and oil in a bowl.

Mix the ingredients together thoroughly, then transfer to a floured working surface. Knead the mixture into a dough with your knuckles.

To make the filling, put the chopped almonds and walnuts in a bowl. In a saucepan, boil together 1 cup/230 ml of water, the honey, sugar, cinnamon, cloves, and nutmeg. Pour the boiling syrup over the nuts and mix well.

Divide the pastry into plum-sized balls. Carefully roll each ball into a flat circle.

Place a little filling in the middle of each circle.

Fold the pastries into semicircles, sealing the edges by pressing down with the fingertips. Arrange the cakes on a baking sheet covered with waxed or silicone paper. Cook in a hot oven (400 °F/200 °C) for 30 minutes. Dust with confectioners' sugar and serve.

Portocalopita

Preparation time: *30 minutes*
Cooking time: *40 minutes*
Difficulty: ★★

Serves 6–8

For the cake:

1 cup/250 ml	virgin olive oil
7/8 cup/200 g	superfine sugar
3	eggs
1	orange
1	lemon
1 tsp/5 g	baking soda
3 7/8 cups/440 g	flour

For the syrup:

4/5 cup/200 ml	orange juice
4/5 cup/200 ml	mandarin juice
1 3/4 cups/200 g	confectioners' sugar

Portocalopita, or "orange cake," is a good example of the type of cakes sold in towns on Crete. As in many Mediterranean cakes and pastries, olive oil is used together with the eggs, citrus fruit juice and zest, and sugar. When cooked, this cake is light and not too sweet. It is generally cut into lozenges and finished with a delicious syrup of orange and mandarin juice.

The use of olive oil is so widespread on Crete that it finds its way into most dishes, even cakes. The island has been known for centuries for its many varieties of olive oil. To make *portocalopita*, the oil is beaten together with the sugar. A good-quality oil will blend with the sugar very quickly. If this does not happen, use an electric beater.

Portocalopita owes its fresh, tangy taste to the citrus fruits used in the recipe. For city-dwelling Cretans, this is a reminder of the countryside in springtime, when the scent of orange blossom perfumes the air. Crete's celebrated Maleme oranges, the island's most famous variety, are grown in the area around Khania. Round and thin-skinned, they are particularly sweet and juicy. They are used as table fruit or for juicing.

Orange trees are relative newcomers to Europe. Unknown to the Greeks and Romans of Antiquity, they were introduced from China in the 15th century by Portuguese explorers. This explains the Greek word for oranges, *portokali*, a corruption of the word for "Portugal."

When they have been cut and soaked in syrup, the pieces of cake can be decorated with slices of citrus fruit and mint leaves. They make an ideal accompaniment to a cup of tea or coffee.

For the cake, begin by pouring most of the olive oil (leaving enough to oil the baking pan) into a bowl. Add the sugar and beat for about 10 minutes until it has dissolved in the oil.

In another bowl, beat the eggs until they are pale yellow and frothy. Add the orange and lemon zest.

Stir the eggs into the oil and sugar mixture and continue beating until all the ingredients are well mixed.

Add the juice of the orange and lemon, together with the baking soda and the flour (leaving a little to flour the baking pan). Mix well. Pour the mixture into the oiled and floured baking pan. Cook in the oven for 35 minutes at 320 °F/160 °C.

To make the syrup, heat the orange and mandarin juice in a pan. Add the confectioners' sugar and mix until it has dissolved.

Take the cake out of the oven and cut it into slices without removing it from the pan. Pour the citrus syrup over the cake and wait until it has been absorbed before turning out the cake. Eat cold.

Pudina Tal-Hobz

Preparation time:	*30 minutes*
Cooking time:	*35 minutes*
Soaking time for bread and dried fruit:	*1 hour*
Resting time for cake:	*24 hours*
Difficulty:	★

Serves 4

2	stale Maltese country bread loaves
3 1/2 tbsp/50 ml	milk
1 stick/120 g	butter
1/5 cup/35 g	candied orange peel
1/5 cup/35 g	candied melon
1/5 cup/35 g	candied figs
1/2 cup/100 g	candied cherries
1 1/2 cups/250 g	raisins
3 cups/350 g	shelled walnuts
4/5 cup/200 ml	dark rum
4/5 cup/200 ml	sweet red vermouth
	grated peel of 1 orange
2 tsp/10 g	ground cinnamon
1/2 tsp/2 1/2 g	ground cloves
2 1/3 cups/530 g	superfine sugar
4 cups/400 g	cocoa powder

Every day on Malta, at four o'clock in the afternoon, people drink tea or coffee, just as they did when the island was under British rule. A slice of *pudina tal-hobz* (meaning "bread pudding") might be eaten at the same time. This rich cake has humble origins as a tasty and economical way of using stale bread in a kind of pudding. As time went by, the pudding was gradually enriched with dried and candied fruits.

The bread used as the basis for this dish is the excellent Maltese *hobza*. Still made in the traditional way, this fine-flavored bread has a soft, white interior and a firm, crisp crust. *Hobza* is extremely popular on Malta. Locals and tourists alike enjoy it as a kind of stuffed sandwich similar to the Provençal *pan bagnat*. For this recipe, after pouring the hot milk and water over the small bread cubes, add the pieces of softened butter immediately, so that they melt in the hot liquid.

We should not be surprised by the large assortment of dried fruits in this cake, since they are all produced by local farmers. Malta has been internationally famous for its oranges for several centuries. At one time, the Knights of Malta sent them to every court in Europe. The sweet oranges, with their thin skins, are juicy and full of flavor, while the bitter (or "Seville") oranges are used for making marmalade, candied peel, and orange flower water.

To make the cake look especially attractive and appetizing when sliced, choose candied fruits of varied and bright colors, making sure that they are well distributed in the mixture.

Cut the bread into small cubes. Place these in a bowl. Add the heated milk, some hot water and then 7 tbsp/100g butter. Leave to soak for 1 hour. Meanwhile, soak the dried and candied fruits, and the chopped nuts in a mixture of rum and vermouth.

Drain the fruit and nut mixture and mix into the rehydrated bread.

To this mixture, add the grated orange peel together with the ground cinnamon and cloves.

Sprinkle most of the sugar over the mixture (reserving enough to sugar the baking pan).

Finally, sprinkle on the cocoa powder. Mix everything thoroughly so that the ingredients are evenly distributed through the mixture.

Spoon the mixture into a greased and sugared baking pan. Cover with a piece of aluminum foil and cook in the oven for 35 minutes at 340 °F/170 °C. Allow the cake to rest for 24 hours before serving in slices.

Oscar's

Preparation time: *50 minutes*
Cooking time: *40 minutes*
Setting time for the orange soup/freezing time for the granita: *12 hours*
Difficulty: ★★

Serves 4

For the lemon ravioli:

5/8 cup/140 g	sugar
2	eggs
	juice of 1 lemon
1½ sticks/150 g	butter
4 sheets	fresh ravioli pasta

For the orange sauce:

3 sheets	gelatin
2/3 cup/150 g	sugar
4 cups/1 liter	orange juice

For the herb liqueur granita:

2 sheets	gelatin
1/4 cup/50 g	sugar
1 2/3 cups/400 ml	Mallorcan herb liqueur

For the garnish (optional):

mint leaves
fresh raspberries
cinnamon sticks
lemon thyme

Oscar Martínez Plaza has based this attractive dessert on typically Balearic ingredients: the filling for the ravioli is flavored with lemons, the sauce is made with oranges, and the granita is full of the fresh aromas of a local herb liqueur. In spring, the mass of blossoming orange, lemon, and almond trees in the Mallorcan countryside is a beautiful sight.

The ravioli can be made with fresh Italian pasta or the Chinese pastry used to make wontons. Alternatively, it can be home-made using 2 5/8 cups/300 g flour, 3 eggs, 2 tbsp/30 ml olive oil, and a pinch of salt. The ingredients are kneaded together into a dough and rolled out until very thin or, if possible, passed through a pasta maker.

The lemon filling is simple to make: the lemon juice should be blended cold with the sugar and eggs and then heated gently until it thickens. Do not try to fill the ravioli until the lemon mixture has cooled down. Allowing half a tablespoonful of filling for each parcel, use a teaspoon to slide it onto the center of each rectangle of pasta.

This dessert is topped with an unusual granita of Mallorcan herb liqueur. Known locally as *licor de hierbas dulces*, it is a beautiful olive green in color. Drunk as a digestif, many Mallorcans make it at home by adding flavorings such as fennel, thyme, rosemary, mint, green walnuts, and coffee beans to an aniseed-based spirit.

Beat the orange sauce with an electric mixer before pouring it over the ravioli. The fresh, contrasting tastes of ravioli, granita, and orange sauce make this an ideal dessert for a summer meal.

First prepare the lemon filling. Beat together the sugar, eggs, and lemon juice in a bowl, then heat gently for about 10 minutes, beating constantly until a thick, smooth cream is obtained.

Allow the lemon mixture to cool to a temperature of 130 °F/55 °C. Now add the butter cut into pieces and mix it in thoroughly as it melts. Leave the mixture to cool.

Briefly cook the pieces of pasta in boiling water, then refresh them with cold water. Drain the pasta and carefully cut each piece in half. Place a tsp of lemon filling on each piece of pasta and fold to make a square shape. Make 8 raviolis like this, then set them aside.

Ravioli

To make the orange sauce, soak the gelatin in a bowl of cold water. Place the sugar and a little water in a saucepan and heat until it caramelizes. Cool it by adding the orange juice. Add the softened gelatin, mixing until it has dissolved. Refrigerate overnight.

To make the granita, first soak the gelatin in cold water. Mix the sugar and herb liqueur together in a saucepan, heating them until they form a syrup. Dilute with 2 cups/500 ml water, then heat again, stirring the mixture.

When it boils, add the softened gelatin, beating with a whisk until it has dissolved. Allow the mixture to cool then freeze overnight at –4 °F/–20 °C. Serve the ravioli on a bed of orange sauce, topped with granita, mint, raspberries, cinnamon sticks, and lemon thyme.

Nonna Narcisa's

Preparation time: *10 minutes*
Cooking time: *5 minutes*
Difficulty: ★

Serves 4

3	oranges
5 tbsp/75 g	superfine sugar
1 lb/500 g	ricotta
1 tsp/5 g	powdered coffee
1 tbsp/30 g	good honey

For the garnish:
mint leaves
orange peel

As a son of Sardinia, Amerigo Murgia has chosen this very simple but delicious dessert featuring ricotta. He spent his childhood in Osini, a mountainous region of the island, and remembers that pastoral life with great fondness. His father was a shepherd, making his own cheese. His mother, Narcisa, prepared this homemade cheese in various and delicious ways.

Today, this dessert based on ricotta is a favorite with Amerigo Murcia's children. Their grandmother, *Nonna* (Grandma) Narcisa, still makes this specialty at home for them. Easy to prepare, it can be served with banana and honey.

The small town of Macomer is a celebrated center for cheese-making on Sardinia. Situated on the edge of the Campeda plateau below the Marghine chain of mountains, this beautiful town has been famous since 1907 (when its first cheese cooperative was set up) for the excellence and variety of its products. Among the local cheeses produced are ricotta, *pecorino sardo*, and the delicately flavored *dolce di Macomer*.

Made using the whey of cow's, sheep's, or ewe's milk, ricotta is frequently used in cooking, for both sweet and savory dishes. Its slightly acidic taste goes wonderfully well with the oranges used in this recipe. Ricotta, meaning "recooked," is a vital ingredient here, and can be found in most good supermarkets and food stores.

Oranges were brought originally from the Far East, and thrive in the sunny Sardinian climate. They are rich in vitamins A and C. The different varieties vary in sweetness, acidity, and flavor. For this recipe, navel oranges, with their particularly juicy flesh, would be ideal.

This delicious dessert is a tribute not only to *Nonna* Narcisa, but also to all Sardinian grandmothers.

Cut 2 of the oranges in half widthwise.

Squeeze the juice from orange halves and remove the pits.

Carefully wash the peel of the third orange. Pare off the peel and cut into fine strips. Cook these in a little water with 4 tbsp of sugar until they are caramelized. Put to one side for the garnish.

Orange Ricotta

Place the ricotta in a bowl and add 1 tbsp of sugar.

Pour the orange juice over the ricotta and mix well.

Place a metal circle on the plate. Fill it with the ricotta mixture. Lift off the circle. Sprinkle the dessert with powdered coffee. Pour over some honey. Garnish with mint leaves and the caramelized orange peel.

Sarikopitès

Preparation time: *20 minutes*
Cooking time: *5 minutes*
Resting time for the pastry: *5 minutes*
Difficulty: ★★

Serves 4

2⅛ cups/250 g	flour
2 tbsp/30 ml	lemon juice
3½ tbsp/50 ml	olive oil
1 pinch	salt
3½ tbsp/50 ml	*tsikoudia* (eau-de-vie)
14 oz/400 g	*xinomyzithra* (Cretan cheese)
	olive oil for frying
10 level tbsp/300 g	thyme honey

Sarikopitès are made in central Crete to celebrate Carnival. They are made from sheets of pastry with a cheese filling, folded over and rolled into a turban shape. The name is derived from the *sariki* or black crocheted caps still worn by some of the older men on Crete.

Ioannis Lappas's recipe enhances the pastry with the flavors of lemon juice and *tsikoudia*, a strong, clear-colored Cretan spirit. Twice-distilled, *tsikoudia* is made from a mixture of cereals and the stalks of grapes, apples, arbutus berries, and herbs (fennel, cilantro, and others).

When the pastry ingredients have been well mixed, form the dough into a flattish ball and leave to rest for 5 minutes. Without this resting period, it will be too rubbery to roll out easily. When it is ready, the pastry is rolled out and cut into strips.

The filling of the *sarikopitès* is simply *xinomyzithra* or "bitter myzithra." This is a creamy, wet, white cheese made on Crete from the whey of ewe's or goat's milk. The whey is heated to a temperature of 156–158 °F/68–70 °C. Fifteen percent of the whole milk is then added, and the heat increased to 197 °F/92 °C. A crust forms on the surface of the milk, which is skimmed off and placed in molds to drain before being salted and pressed in cloth bags. The cheese is then put into barrels to mature for two months. For this recipe, you can also use *brousse*, made from ewe's milk, ricotta, or feta blended with lemon juice and some salt and pepper.

When the *sarikopitès* have been cooked to a golden brown, a generous serving of honey is drizzled over them. Grape syrup or a sprinkling of sugar can be used if preferred.

Put the flour in a bowl and add the lemon juice, olive oil, salt, tsikoudia, *and 1 cup/250 ml water. Knead well with the fingertips, then shape the dough into a ball. Pull it out into a sausage shape and flatten slightly. Leave it to rest for 5 minutes.*

Roll the pastry out thinly. Cut it into strips approximately 16 inches/40 cm by 2 inches/4–5 cm.

Place a line of xinomyzithra *along each strip of pastry.*

with Honey

Roll each strip lengthwise around the filling, then coil the rolls around themselves like a snail shell.

Deep fry the pastries for about 5 minutes in a pan of oil. Drain them on paper towels.

Drizzle honey over the sarikopitès *and serve them warm.*

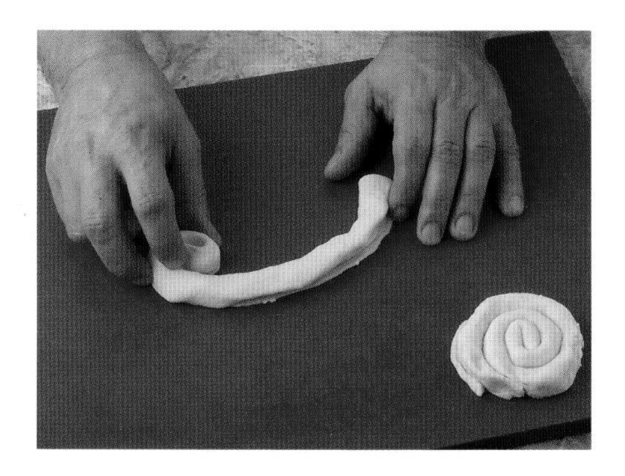

Apricot Soup with Terrine

Preparation time:	*40 minutes*
Cooking time:	*45 minutes*
Cooling time for terrine:	*3–4 hours*
Difficulty:	★★

Serves 4

For the terrine:

$^{2}/_{3}$ cup/150 ml	milk
$^{1}/_{3}$ cup/75 g	sugar
$^{2}/_{3}$ cup/150 ml	light cream
5 oz/150 g	egg yolks
2 sheets	gelatin
	grated peel of 1 lemon
1 tsp/5 g	ground cinnamon
1 cup/200 g	fromage frais (or 1 cup cream cheese beaten together with $^{1}/_{4}$ cup lemon juice)

For the apricot soup:

$1^{3}/_{4}$ lb/800 g	fresh apricots
$^{2}/_{3}$ cup/150 g	sugar
$^{4}/_{5}$ cup/200 ml	triple-sec (orange liqueur)
1 cup/250 ml	orange juice

For the garnish (optional):

chocolate
fresh mint leaves
red berries (any variety)

The inhabitants of the Balearic Islands enjoy desserts made of mild, fresh cheeses served with honey, sprinkled with sugar, and brûléed. Many types of fruit are grown on the islands, and another favorite dessert consists of apricots toasted on a flat sheet of heated metal called a *plancha*. In this recipe, Bartolomé-Jaime Trias Luis first toasts the apricots in this way, then cooks them in a mixture of caramel, triple-sec, and orange juice. Finally, he blends the ingredients together in a food processor. The resulting "soup" has a wonderful color and taste, its sweetness offsetting the slightly acid cheese.

The cheese terrine is a mixture of a light custard flavored with grated lemon peel and cinnamon, gelatin, and cream cheese. The mixture is poured into individual molds and placed in the refrigerator to cool. When set, the terrines can be easily slid out of the molds by dipping the bottoms of the containers into a bowl of hot water.

Apricots are one of the major fruit crops on the Balearic Islands. For this recipe, they can be toasted on top of the stove, in a metal pan, or browned in the oven. In all cases, they should be carefully watched, as they burn easily.

The apricot soup is given added flavor with the addition of orange juice and triple-sec. This is a liqueur made of orange peel, generally drunk with ice or used as an ingredient in cocktails, fruit salads, and ice creams. Kirsch makes a good substitute if triple-sec is unobtainable. When the apricots have been thoroughly cooked in this fragrant mixture of liquids, they are blended in a food processor. They should be sieved after this to remove any bits of skin.

Pour some apricot soup into each plate. Place a terrine in the middle, decorated with some halved blackberries and a mint leaf. Reserve a few apricots, and add these as a garnish together with a few blueberries.

To make the cheese terrine, heat the milk, sugar, and cream in a saucepan. Beat the egg yolks in a bowl. Pour a little warm milk over the eggs, then add them to the saucepan. Heat gently until the mixture thickens. Remove from the heat and add the softened gelatin.

Add the grated lemon peel and cinnamon to the custard, then carefully mix in the cheese. Pour the mixture into individual molds. Leave these to cool for 3 or 4 hours.

To make the apricot soup, cut the apricots in half and remove the pits. Toast them on both sides in a very hot pan.

# of Cream Cheese

Heat the sugar with a little water until it caramelizes. When it is a pale golden color, add the toasted apricots.

Pour the triple-sec over the fruit. Cook rapidly for about 10 minutes, stirring so that the apricots do not stick.

Add the orange juice. Cover the saucepan and simmer for 10 minutes. Set aside 2 or 3 apricots, blending the rest in a food processor. Leave to cool. Surround each terrine with the soup. Decorate with quartered apricots, mint, and red berries.

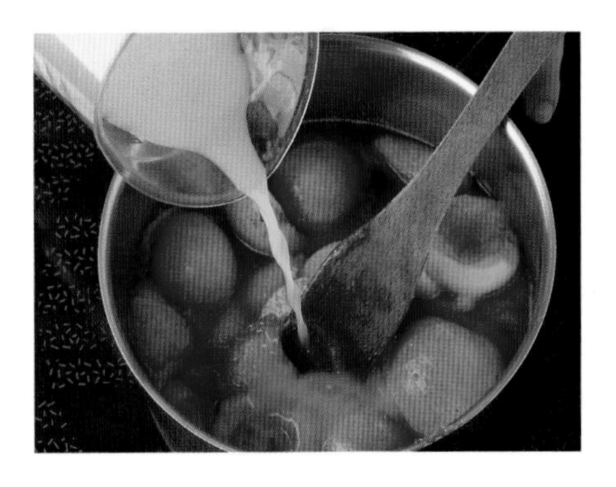

The Chefs

Giuseppe Barone
Sicily

Michael Cauchi
Malta

Johann Chetcuti
Malta

Serge Fazzini
Corsica

Ioannis Lappas
Crete

Angelo La Spina
Sicily

Michalis Markakis
Crete

Oscar Martínez Plaza
Balearic Islands

Amerigo Murgia
Sardinia

Vincent Tabarani
Corsica

Bartolomé-Jaime Trias Luis
Balearic Islands

Abbreviations:

1 oz = 1 ounce = 28 grams
1 lb = 1 pound = 16 ounces
1 cup = 8 ounces *(see below)
1 cup = 8 fluid ounces = 250 ml (liquids)
2 cups = 1 pint (liquids)
1 glass = 4–6 fluid ounces = 125–150 ml (liquids)
1 tbsp = 1 level tablespoon = 15–20 g *(see below) = 15 ml (liquids)
1 tsp = 1 level teaspoon = 3–5 g *(see below) = 5 ml (liquids)

1 kg = 1 kilogram = 1000 grams
1 g = 1 gram = 1/1000 kilogram
1 l = 1 liter = 1000 milliliters = approx. 34 fluid ounces
1 ml = 1 milliliter = 1/1000 liter

*The weight of dry ingredients varies significantly depending on the density factor, e.g. 1 cup flour weighs less than 1 cup butter.
Quantities in ingredients have been rounded up or down for convenience, where appropriate. Metric conversions may therefore not correspond exactly.
It is important to use either American or metric measurements within a recipe.

Design and production: Fabien Bellahsen and Daniel Rouche
Photographs and technical direction: Didier Bizos
Photographic Assistants: Hasni Alamat and Morgane Favennec
Editors: Élodie Bonnet, Nathalie Talhouas
Assistant Editors: Fabienne Ripon

Thanks to:
Crete:
Andonis Panayotopoulos, President of the Greek Academy of Taste
Nikos Psilakis, Vice-President of the Greek Academy of Taste
Nikos Skoulas, Honorary President of the Greek Academy of Taste, Former Minister of Tourism
Yannis Patellis, President of the Greek National Tourist Office
Grecotel and Istron Bay Hotel
With the generous collaboration of Maria Stephanides, Hellenic Agricultural Insurance Organization (ELGA)

Malta:
Dr Michael Refalo, Minister of Tourism, Malta
Dominiç Micallef, Regional Director (Southern Europe), Maltese Tourist Office in France

Original title: *Délices des Îles de Méditerranée*

ISBN of the original edition: 2-8469-0063-9
ISBN of the German edition: 3-8331-2334-6

Translation from French:
Caroline Higgitt for Cambridge Publishing Management Limited
Edited by Louise Lalaurie-Rogers for Cambridge Publishing Management Limited
Proofread by Karolin Thomas for Cambridge Publishing Management Limited
Typeset and managed by Cambridge Publishing Management Limited

Project Coordinator: Isabel Weiler

Printed in Germany

ISBN 3-8331-2335-4

10 9 8 7 6 5 4 3 2 1
X IX VIII VII VI V IV III II I